Behind the Paranormal 2:

Bigfoot, Mothman and Monsters You Never Heard of

Paul Eno | Ben Eno

Cover illustration by RikoBest/Shutterstock
Featuring original artwork by Karin Mansberg
Interior illustrations as credited
Cover and interior design by New River Press
Type set in Blue Highway Linocut/Minion Pro/Tahoma

Published by Barking Cat Books
An Imprint of New River Press
645 Fairmount St., Woonsocket, RI 02895
(888) 273-1941
books@newriverpress.com

NewRiverPress.com

Library of Congress Cataloging in Publication Data applied for.

ISBN 978-1-891724-20-6

Visit father-son authors and broadcasters Paul & Ben Eno at
Behindtheparanormal.com
and Newenglandghosts.com

First Revised Edition, July 2017
Printed in the United States of America

An Imprint of New River Press

To Jonathan

Beloved Son, Brother and Friend

CONTENTS

The Monster Hunters: Loren Coleman 9

Introduction: MONSTERS? 10

The World of 'Cryptids' 10
Where do they come from and where do they go? 12
Electricity, Space and Time 14
Creatures of the 'Multiverse'? 14
Into the 'Flap Area' 15
Reality vs. Reality Shows 17

Chapter 1: BIGFOOT 19

The Monster Hunters: Shane Sirois 21
Bigfoot Banter? 24
A Paranormal Pickup? 24
Something Big 24
A Thing Between the Trees 25
The Big Guy has many names 25
The Patterson-Gimlin Film 25
The Monster Hunters: Jeff Hilling 26
Two Legs or Four? 28
The Mystery of Panther Rock 28
The Monster Hunters: Philip Spencer 29
The Population Question 30
Bigfoot's European Cousins 31
A Man-Shaped Hole in Reality 33
Weirdness in the Big Thicket 33
The Monster Hunters: Rob Riggs 34

Those Orbs Again 34
A Deafening Howl 35
Bigfoot in the North Carolina Mountains 37
The Monster Hunters: Tom Burnette 38
Monsterland 39
The Monster Hunters: Ronny LeBlanc 40
The Woonsocket Wild Man? 43
The Nasty Almasty 45
The Monster Hunters: Richard Freeman 45
What is Bigfoot? 46

Chapter 2: Mothman 47

The Monster Hunters: Jeff Wamsley 50
The Monster Hunters: Susan Sheppard 51
Footsteps on the Roof 52
Sightings into the 1990s 53
What is Mothman? 54
MIB Mischief 54
Treated for Shock 55
Collapse of the Silver Bridge 56
Other Explanations for Mothman 57
Jeff's Interpretation 57
Who's on First? 57
The Monster Hunters: Robin Bellamy 58
A Strange, High-Pitched Wailing 59
The Coming of Indrid Cold 60
A flap in more ways than one? 61
An eyewitness appears on our show 62
What does Mothman really look like? 63
Is Mothman really a precursor of disaster? 63
Is Mothman just the icing on the cake? 64
How accurate were reports about the MIBs? 65
Still Kicking 65
Helped by Mothman? 65
More Blessings from Mothman 66
As we go to press.... 66
Behind Our Folklore 67

Chapter 3: CANINE CRYPTIDS 69

A California Wolfman 71
The Michigan Dogman 71
The Beast of Bray Road 72
The Monster Hunters: Linda Godfrey 74
Another Multiversal Creature? 75
'Gadara' 75
About Those Hind Legs 76
Not Very Human 78
Linda Godfrey's Own Sighting 79

Chapter 4: SEA AND LAKE MONSTERS 80

Blackie makes an appearance 82
A Chinese River Monster? 83
The Great New England Sea Serpent 83
A Surfeit of Serpents 85
The Monster Hunters: Jeremy Robinson 85
Meg 86
The Monster Hunters: Steve Alten 87
The Sea vs. the Lake 89
Nessie and Champ 89
The Monster Hunters: Nick Redfern 90
Where do they come from and how do they survive? 91
Even in Little Lakes 91
Monsters and the Military 92
Lake Monsters as Military Decoys? 93
Champ 93
Lexie 95
The Flathead Lake Monster 95
What are they? 96
Hoaxes and Blurry Photos 97

Chapter 5: Humanoids 98

The Multiverse Revisited? 99
A Beard and a Helmet 99
The Monster Hunters: Albert Rosales 100
Albert's Weirdest Cases 101
Could they have been mechanical or biomechanical? 101

The Flying Humanoids 103
A Real Bruhaha in Mexico 103
Multiple Witnesses in St. Louis 104
Separating Fact from Fancy 104
Paul meets the fairies – almost 104
The Repeaters 105
Fairies are one thing. But 'pukwudgies'? 106
The Copicut Reservoir Beings 106
Paul & Ben photograph...what? 106
Mermaids 109
The Monster Hunters: Wahaba Hadia al Mu'id 109
A Worldwide Phenomenon 112
A Merboy? 113
More Aquatic Humanoids 113
Humanoids in Cave Paintings 114
The Butterfly People of Joplin 115

Chapter 6: Out of Place Animals 116

One Step Ahead of the Law 118
From Old England to New England 119
The Peduzzi Sighting, 1946 120
On the Appalachian Trail 120
The Mansfield Mystery Cat 121
Rattled Raccoons 122
The Evidence 122
No Pouch Potatoes Here 123
The Kangaroo from Hell 125

Chapter 7: Monsters You Never Heard Of 126

Goatman Butts In 127
Monkeying Around 128
El Chupacabras 128
The Mongolian Death Worm 129
The Orang Pendek 132
The Batsquatch of Tacoma 132
The Ear Eater of Jasper County 134
A Tough-Toothed Lizardman in South Carolina 134
Lizard Liaison 136

The Owlman 136
The Jersey Devil 137
Anything Weird that Flies 139
The Webb Lake Big Bird 139
The Black Hawk Connection 140
The Van Meter Visitor 142
Back to the Multiverse Yet Again? 142

Epilogue 143
Should we be afraid? 145
Has mainstream science loosened up on cryptids? 146
Talk to the animals 146
Does it really depend on who's looking? 147
Nice Doggie 147
Bibliography 149
The Authors: Paul & Ben Eno 152
The Illustrator: Karin Mansberg 154
Other Books by Paul & Ben Eno 154
Books by Paul F. Eno 154
Acknowledgements 155

Visit the International Cryptozoology Museum 158

Visit the Mothman Museum 159

The Monster Hunters

Loren Coleman

It's impossible to write a book on cryptids without paying homage to the undisputed dean of cryptozoologists, Loren Coleman.

Born in Norfork, Virginia, in 1947, Loren has lived in Illinois, California, Massachusetts and Maine, and he has investigated cryptozoological evidence and folklore since the Abominable Snowmen caught his interest in 1960.

Loren is the author, coauthor, editor, and/or contributor of, or to, over 100 popular books on natural history mysteries and the media. These include 40 books of his own, such as *The Field Guide to Lake Monsters and Sea Serpents*, *The Field Guide to Bigfoot and Other Mystery Primates*, *Mysterious America*, *Bigfoot!: The True Story of Apes in America*, *Cryptozoology A to Z*, *The Copycat Effect*, *Tom Slick and the Search for the Yeti*, and *Mothman and Other Curious Encounters.* Loren has been involved in writing introductions, chapters and prefaces for 60 other books. He regularly appears on, and consults to, documentary television programs, including *MonsterQuest, In Search Of, Mysteries at the Museum, CBS News Sunday Morning, Unsolved Mysteries, Animal X, Ancient Aliens, Ancient Mysteries*, and many other media.

Loren Coleman
Photo Courtesy Loren Coleman/Int. Cryptozoology Museum

Loren taught at six New England universities from 1980 through 2003 (in sociology, anthropology, social work and documentary film), and was a full-time senior researcher at the Muskie School of Public Policy at the University of Southern Maine from 1983-2006. He belongs to a number of presigious organizations, and he travels extensively to continue his field work and lectures.

The author of two daily blogs, Loren in 2003 founded the nonprofit, 501(c)3 International Cryptozoology Museum in Portland, Maine (see page 149). It is the world's only cryptozoology museum to be routinely recognized by global media. Find out more at http://www.imdb.com/name/nm0171129/ and http://www.cryptozoologymuseum.com.

MONSTERS?

As heard on
CBS Radio - August 22, 2010
WOON 1240 Radio – January 5, 2015, April 10, 2016

In the 2002 movie *The Mothman Prophecies*, this telephone exchange takes place between newspaper reporter John Klein (played by Richard Gere) and the creepy voice of the mysterious Indrid Cold.

KLEIN: "What do you look like?"

COLD: "It depends on who's looking."

When it comes to people who encounter "monsters," dear old Indrid might have been more correct than he realized. The kinds of bizarre, extinct or unheard-of creatures that people report seeing or hearing can be as many and varied as the people who encounter them. In fact, some people report being completely terrified during their experience. Others say they felt privileged, and sometimes even blessed by something sacred.

Doesn't this mean that people are just imagining these creatures? Or are they just mistaken about what they see and hear? In some cases, "yes" is the answer to one or both questions, but not in every case. In many encounters, there's more than one eyewitness and, in some instances, there's physical evidence, such as footprints, photographs, audio recordings or even hair and blood samples.

So, can there really be monsters? People are certainly encountering something strange. Maybe the very term "monster" provokes disbelief, preventing many people from looking further for answers.

The World of 'Cryptids'

Linda Godfrey (Page 74) is the author of 17 books on strange creatures, phenomena and people, and she's a respected researcher into the weird world of "cryptids." Like Paul Eno, co-author of this book, Linda has had a long career as an investigative journalist.

"'Monster' implies something that isn't right: Something that's too big, might frighten you, eat you, and perhaps has fangs and a fearsome appearance," Linda told us during one of her many interviews on our weekly radio show, *Behind the Paranormal with Paul & Ben Eno.*

The show was heard on CBS Radio in Boston, Detroit, Pittsburgh and Seattle from 2009 to 2014, and now has a noontime destination radio slot on WOON 1240 AM in the Providence/Boston market.

Linda joined us on CBS Radio on February 6, 2011.

"The term 'monsters,' and the experiences that accompany encounters with them, encompass a broad range, from ancient and legendary creatures to things that go about by air, land and sea," she explained.

She pointed out three main types of mystery animal.

"The first are simple. They are 'cryptids,' species of animals whose existence is unrecognized by mainstream science," she explained.

"The second are quasi- or pseudo-cryptids. The animals in this group are a little more problematical, as they are members of a species that's known to exist, but are being found in a place where they aren't supposed to be. This can be because they're presumed to be extinct in that specific area or, more commonly, because they're an exotic species, and some individuals have escaped or been re-introduced."

These are sometimes called out-of-place animals or "animal erratics."

"The third, final and, in some ways, most contentious of the three groupings of apparently unknown creatures are the ones that may well not be creatures at all," at least not in the normal, physical sense of the word.

Linda has had a lifelong interest in strange occurrences. As a young reporter for a Wisconsin newspaper, "I felt that, if there really are strange, predatory animals prowling around the woods, fields and backyards of the United States,

What is a cryptid?

Cryptozoology is the study of animals that might or might not exist, especially legendary animals like Bigfoot and the Loch Ness monster. These unknown animals are known as cryptids. The mainstream academic world does not recognize cryptozoology as a real science.

people have a right to know," she said.

"What if there's an explanation…that these aren't real and that something totally unknown and bizarre is making people insist they're seeing these things?"

In her books, Linda presents cryptid reports from "sober, credible people, many of whom don't want their names used because they don't want their neighbors and friends to make fun of them."

"They see these creatures. What I hear over and over from people who've contacted me for going on 23 years now, is that they're really happy to find someone who will listen to them and not tell them they're crazy."

In fact, there's very little that witnesses can tell Linda that she hasn't heard already. But how does she tell the difference between a credible report and a hoax?

"I really try to vet every report that comes to me," Linda explained. "Some are easy. 'I saw a 10-foot werewolf in the cemetery last night.' I reject anything that has a mocking tone."

Then there are reports that are too vague to take seriously.

"'I saw something brown and furry between the trees.' I'll ask, 'Did you see a face or ears?' If the answer is 'no,' what they saw could have been anything. This might be a very sincere and credible person, but there's just not enough to it."

Linda also receives "super-dramatic reports, where people are giving me these crazy, minute details, and things I've never heard before. Like the guy who happened to be in a cemetery at night and happened to have a silver lance, struck the creature in the eye, and green ooze flowed out. No, thanks."

Stories like these are in the minority, Linda said.

"Ninety percent of the reports I get are from sincere and credible people. Daylight sightings are better than nighttime sightings because there's greater detail. Some witnesses are right out in the field with the cryptid, while others are zooming by in their cars. There are a lot of variables," she added.

"Consistency of accounts among witnesses isn't necessarily a factor, because different people notice different things,"

Where do they come from and where do they go?

If even some of these cryptids are real, the question arises: How could a creature as large as Bigfoot or a lake monster, or as weird as an "upright canine cryptid," remain hidden in the modern world?

"Cryptids seem to have an elusive quality, the apparent ability to foul up electrical equipment, or at least to sense it and stay off of it. And I don't know why. Some people think they inhabit old mines or caves, where they would be difficult to find," Linda stated.

"I often make the comparison with bears. They're elusive. If a bear doesn't

What is the multiverse?

- The multiverse is one term for the elegant, interactive system of multiple universes that make up reality, according to many interpretations of theoretical physics. One interpretation is:
- All possible worlds, and all possible creatures, actually exist in physical reality.
- They regularly interact through intersects and overlaps.
- Most parallel worlds have different laws of physics, creating entirely different levels of awareness.
- Different versions of each life form, including ourselves, exist in many worlds,
- People who have died here are alive in many parallel worlds.
- Quantum effects explain all paranormal activity.

Bruce Rolff/Shutterstock

want you to see it, you probably won't. Yet, if a bear shows up in someone's backyard, you can bet the TV news reporters will be there, taking photos and videos of it."

Linda made a crucial point: Unlike most cryptid photos, pictures of the bears are usually crisp and clear.

"The bear may be on the ground or in a tree, but the photos and videos don't go gray or turn blurry. They're clear as day for all to see. That doesn't happen with cryptids, and I have no explanation for why that occurs."

There are tracks attributed to cryptids, especially Bigfoot, but sometimes these will begin and end abruptly, often leading to hoax suspicions. There are reports of cryptids appearing and/or disappearing right on front of people, sometimes with multiple witnesses.

Electricity, Space and Time

"Cars suddenly stopping seems to be a very common happening during encounters with high strangeness" like cryptids, Linda noted.

Witnesses sometimes report missing time, and a strong feeling of being out of place. Electronics and machinery often quit, as if hit by an electromagnetic pulse (EMP). In fact, paranormal "flap areas," as we call them, often exist in areas of geological or gravitational irregularities, such as the Bouguer Anomaly, a strange phenomenon in which terrain affects gravity, sometimes decreasing it.

Other than the occasional set of tracks, physical evidence for cryptids usually is limited to hair samples and, rarely, blood.

"When tested, these samples only show the DNA and hair morphology. It can't prove that a canine cryptid walks upright or has elongated paws," Linda stated.

Creatures of the 'Multiverse'?

The co-authors of this book have a possible explanation for why cryptids are so elusive, why very little credible physical evidence of them is ever found, why no-one has ever recovered a dead cryptid, as far as we know, and an explanation even for the anomalous tracks and sightings.

We call it the "multiverse." We explain this concept in detail in the first book in this series, *Behind the Paranormal: Everything You Know is Wrong* (Schiffer Publishing, 2016).

Essentially, as indicated in the bizarre science of quantum physics, there might not be just the one universe that most of us experience, but many parallel and interacting universes. Perhaps there are an infinite number. What's more, the laws of physics may be different – sometimes a little, sometimes a lot – from universe to universe. Further, all possible possibilities may exist in this elegantly interactive multiverse. That includes so-called monsters like Bigfoot and the rest of the menagerie that people report seeing from time to time and in certain places.

As a paranormal researcher in the 1970s, Paul ran into experiencers who were seeing ghosts not only of people who were still alive, but ghosts of themselves. Others reported appearing and disappearing buildings. Paul himself encountered other phenomena that were far too big and complex to be contained by the old ideas of a "spirit world."

We believe that not only what we call ghosts, but UFOs, cryptids and virtually all things paranormal result from overwashes, intersects and overlaps between both our family of very similar parallel worlds (which may contain other versions of ourselves) and worlds that aren't so similar.

If the boundaries (or "branes," as physicists call them) between these parallel worlds really are electromagnetic and plasma-charged, as many speculate, it could easily explain the blurry photos of cryptids, UFOs and ghosts, as taken from our side of the brane. And it could easily explain the electromagnetic anomalies that affect electronic equipment and cars.

We go even further. We believe that, during paranormal encounters, experiencers are partially or even fully across the brane themselves. The encounter takes place not only because the cryptid's (or ghost's, alien's or UFO's) world is intersecting ours, but because ours is intersecting theirs. Sometimes the consequences are unpredictable.

The multiverse scenario raises entirely new questions, such as: What do we mean by "real"? What constitutes proof or even evidence? Is our old, materialist paradigm, on which the whole scientific method is based, even valid anymore? While the disciplined thinking that science can bring to any field, especially one as slippery as the paranormal, is essential, how far will it actually go in providing validity?

Researchers like Linda Godfrey are very open to the multiverse idea as an explanation for some or even most cryptids.

"This theory explains all that, especially the issues with photography, the coming and going of cryptids, and the lack of physical evidence. It's a lot more likely than people changing into werewolves," Linda declared.

Into the 'Flap Area'

In our experience, the multiverse idea also explains flap areas, regions of frequent but seemingly unrelated paranormal activity, including ghost and poltergeist phenomena, UFOs, dislocations in time and space and, of course, cryptids. We believe that flap areas occur because they contain unusually high numbers of intersects and overlaps among our world and many parallel worlds.

This resonates with Linda Godfrey. Asked if she finds other kinds of paranormal phenomena in areas where cryptids are operating....

"Yes, I find this time and time again. UFOs seem to be the most common phenomenon (accompanying cryptid reports). I like to map things out, to get a handle on what's going on throughout a given area," Linda said.

"Sometimes there are major power lines. I also look at maps to see what geographical, geological, and human cultural artifacts are present in areas where sightings take place. Very often, I'll find Native American sites, reservations and sacred lands."

At times of sightings, Linda also looks for reports of concurrent solar flares and moon phases, along with UFO and Bigfoot reports.

"I've never found any real correlation between upright canines and full moons," she quipped.

So much for werewolf folklore. In fact, the three-quarter moon shows up more than any other phase during canine cryptid sightings, according to Linda.

One flap area she has identified is the "Jefferson County Square of Weirdness" in Wisconsin. There are ancient Native American burial mounds, reports of canine cryptids, giant birds and Bigfoot, all within 13 square miles.

One of the first weird encounters (that we know of) in this area took place in 1936 and involved a night watchman and a large, upright canine cryptid digging in a Native American burial mound in the middle of the night. The creature evidently attempted to communicate with the human (page 72).

Within this Square of Weirdness, there's Rock Lake, with pyramids on its bottom, not to mention Rocky the Lake Monster. There's a "ghost road" where people report seeing giant birds. And this was a center of the Aztalan or Mississippian native culture, also known as the Mound Builders (hence the pyramids). There are unusual native burials, where people report seeing visions, and there also are reports of people or ghosts dressed in very old deerskin clothing.

Native Americans have their own opinions about cryptids but, in our view, these also add up to the multiverse, explained in their own ancient terms. To the First Nations, creatures like Bigfoot and the Dogman are actually "spirit creatures" that come and go from what amount to parallel worlds. We wonder: Did the natives consider flap areas sacred because they knew there were intersects with other worlds, gateways for what they considered supernatural beings? We believe they did because their traditions tell us so.

"They just know where the 'doors' are," explained Linda. "When cryptids are here, they're fully physical. They can eat and interact. Then they can go back to their own worlds. That's why we never find bodies."

Linda took it all one step further.

"If a cryptid comes from a parallel world that isn't too dissimilar (to ours), it could be based a few steps up the electromagnetic ladder, perhaps at a different literal vibration," Linda continued.

"Our trail cams might not be built to their specifications. So, we might not be able to fully capture things that are physical in our own realm, but are a few notches up or down on that electromagnetic ladder. They don't register correctly on our equipment."

Why do only certain people seem to encounter cryptids? Robin Bellamy (page

57), a Canadian cryptid researcher who grew up in West Virginia and believes she saw Mothman as a child, has an opinion.

"People start noticing these things more once they've experienced one of them. If you've witnessed what you believe is a UFO, for instance, that profoundly changes you as a person. I believe it also makes you a little more willing to see other phenomena that might be occurring at the same time," Robin said during our radio interview.

"It's not that there's an increase in activity, there's an increase in awareness."

Robin noted that the Point Pleasant, West Virginia, area and the Ohio River Valley, where most of the Mothman activity took place in the 1960s, is in the Rome Trough, an area of strange geology that includes the Bouguer Anomaly and runs from roughly Pittsburgh, Pennsylvania, to Louisville, Kentucky.

"Ordinarily, the closer you get to the center of the Earth, the more intense the gravity. In this case, it's the other way around. The deeper you get into that trough, the lighter the gravity. This is very much a coal and gas area, and there has been much geological study," Robin stated.

In our experience, gravity anomalies can join electromagnetic effects in playing tricks with space and time – with the branes that join one parallel universe to another.

Reality vs. Reality Shows

Despite the scientific innuendoes of cryptid encounters, who is doing the research, and how credible are they? The kinds of people who research cryptids range from folks with actual training as biologists and/or zoologists, like Richard Freeman of the prestigious Centre for Fortean Zoology (page 43), to hobbyists and pop researchers with no real qualifications. While some television "reality shows" are better than others, most are ruled by the pop researchers. Unfortunately, these shows are where most people get their information about cryptids.

It's important to remember that reality shows are entertainment, not science.

Asked how informative or accurate the reality shows are when it comes to cryptids, Linda Godfrey shared our skepticism.

"Reality shows are reliably inaccurate," said Linda, who has appeared in some of the more credible documentary series, such as *MonsterQuest* on the History Channel.

"They want a sensational story, and sometimes the facts aren't quite sensational enough for them. They sometimes blur the characteristics of a creature to make it seem like something else."

Reality-show producers do a lot of creative cutting and pasting, said Linda.

"I've seen shows that will pull in totally unrelated clips from other shows about different topics, and make them seem as if they're part of it. So, if you're only getting your cryptozoology from TV, you're getting a very skewed picture," she declared.

"There are even shows where the so-called investigators are just paid actors, going out and looking silly. They go out, make noise, and they hear bumps and bangs in the forest that might be anything."

Serious investigators "go out, spend the time and do it properly," Linda said.

Robin Bellamy (Page 58) agrees with us that, when it comes to the paranormal in general and cryptids in particular, it's still the first day of school.

"Do cryptids have an agenda or purpose? Beware of attributing human motivations to what amount to alien beings," said Robin.

"We're dealing with something we know nothing about, and it's very arrogant to think we know their agenda, if there is one. It's a matter of perspective. We have to start being open to possibilities beyond conventional science."

Now, let's go meet some cryptids.

As heard on

CBS Radio – November 22, 2009
WOON 1240 Radio – May 2, 2011, October 27, 2014, April 23, 2017

The rural Pennsylvania sky was brilliantly moonlit on the chilly night of Friday, September 16, 2016. Paul Eno, co-author of this book, sat in his pickup truck at the edge of a hilltop field in the farm country outside the small city of Dubois. Paul had been there for over two hours, and he was looking for strange lights in the sky, something he and his colleague, Shane Sirois (see page 21), had photographed over this field four months before.

"I was in my truck with the driver's-side window down," Paul recalled. "At about 10 p.m., I heard a snuffling about 20 feet to the left, under an old deer stand that had been overtaken by grape vines. Then there was a heavy exhale, as from a bull or horse."

Paul realized that this might very well be a bear, as they are abundant in this part of western Pennsylvania.

"The moon was full, and the entire five-acre field in my line of sight was very well lit. I was watching the deer stand to see if anything, bear or otherwise, would emerge," said Paul.

"Suddenly, something made me look to the right. Through the closed passenger-side window, at a point we later found was about 200 feet to my right, I was stunned to see a very large, brown, hairy, upright someone or something, clearly walking."

Paul was adamant that this was a two-legged creature.

"I could see the two massive knees moving up and down through the tall grass. Its head was bowed as if it were looking for something."

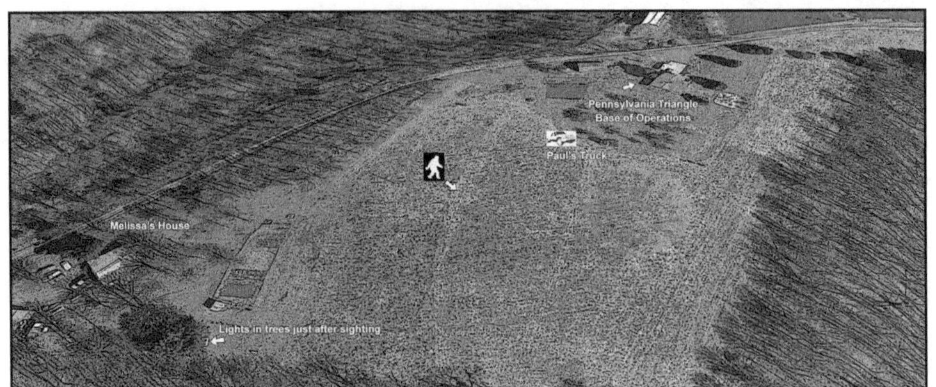

Above is an annotated aerial photo of the Pennsylvania field where Paul Eno believes he sighted a Bigfoot on the night of September 16, 2016. Below is the abortive infrared photo Paul took out the window of his truck.

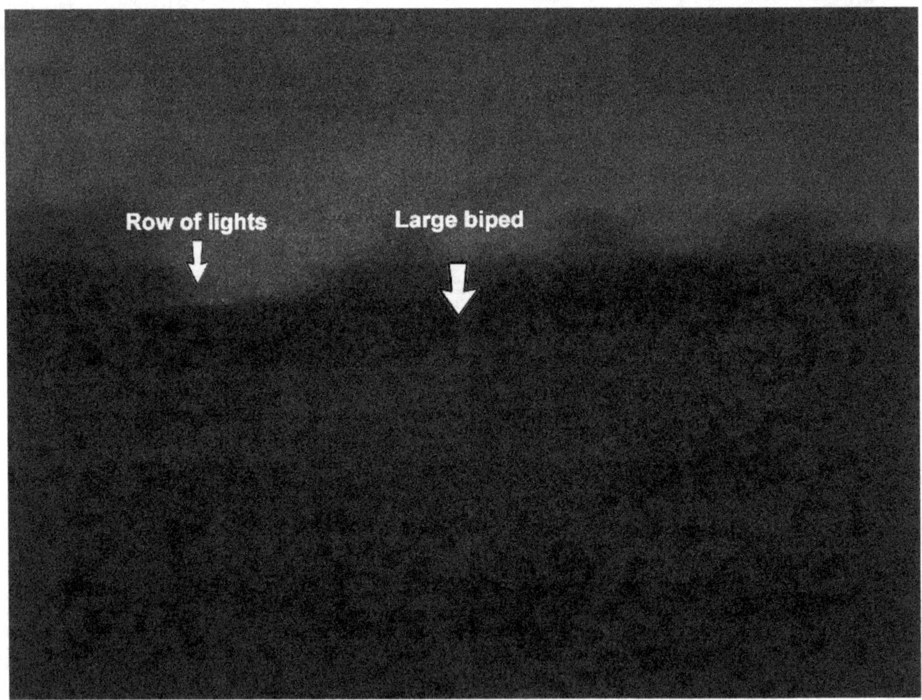

Paul desperately snapped an infrared photo through the closed, cold passenger-side window. Of course, there was no heat signature and, therefore, no recognizable image of the creature. So, Paul opened the door and left the truck as quietly as he could.

"As I raised the camera to take (the picture on the next page), in an achievement of bad timing that should remain infamous in the annals of the paranor-

The Monster Hunters

Shane Sirois

Shane Sirois

As described by Paul Eno, Shane Sirois is a Blackfoot shaman and a "feet-on-the-ground paranormal investigator - a very good combination." He is one of the few fellow paranormal researchers the authors will work with.

Paul first met Shane in 1998 during a Rhode Island ghost case, and was amazed to find that the New Hampshire investigator had arrived at the same conclusions about the paranormal being a byproduct of multiverse reality, and "demons" actually being inter-world parasites.

Now Paul, Ben and Shane work on flap area cases together, and Shane regularly co-hosts open-line shows on *Behind the Paranormal with Paul & Ben Eno*. Their work together has brought them into contact with UFOs, Bigfoot and other cryptids. Shane has been working in the paranormal field for over 30 years, and he has a 100 percent success rate when it comes to helping people rid themselves of paranormal parasites.

"Because of his great work in flap areas, Shane has had Bigfoot experiences and can now be considered a monster hunter with the best of them," Paul said.

His website: Trueghost.com

Shane Sirois (arrow) retraces the steps of the creature seen by Paul Eno, and apparently heard by neighbor Melissa and her daughter, on the night of September 16, 2016, in a field at the heart of the "Pennsylvania Triangle."

mal, my wife called!"

As Paul's ring tone, the "Shire Theme" from *The Lord of the Rings* movies, blasted through the night, the whatever-it-was had already disappeared.

"I know -- I should have had the phone turned off or on vibrate. But who was going to call me in the middle of the night in a Pennsylvania field? It was the closest I've ever come to filing for divorce. I slunk back into the truck."

But this wasn't the end of what Paul believed to be his first Bigfoot sighting.

"Only a few minutes later, a spotlight from the ground shot up into some trees at the far edge of the field. It moved around, then illuminated the base of the tree," Paul said. "I wanted to take off after it, but I wasn't sure about the terrain in this field when it came to driving."

The following evening, Paul and Shane presided over a meeting of people from this

The track of a large, bipedal creature, found on September 17, 2016, after Paul's sighting of the night before.

Shane points out where he saw a large, hairy bipedal creature on May 21, 2016, in woods adjacent to a Pennsylvania cornfield. Shane is six feet tall, and he said that the creature's head reached as high as the sign, making it roughly eight feet tall.

A 15-inch barefoot print found by Paul and Shane in the Pennsylvania Triangle, May 21, 2016.

area, which they were already calling the "Pennsylvania Triangle." Nearly 20 people turned out, all of whom reported paranormal experiences in the area.

"Shane and I made a presentation on our paranormal theories and methods, and why we believed that these folks were living in a paranormal hotspot or flap area, as we call it."

When Paul related his apparent Bigfoot encounter from the night before, and got to the part about seeing lights shining up into a tree, a woman raised her hand.

"That was me and my daughter," said the woman, Melissa, who lived in the house just beyond the field. "We had just come home, and we heard something big moving around in that field. We took our flashlights and went to see what it was."

Asked why she pointed the light into the tree, Melissa responded that Bigfoot and similar creatures in the area had sometimes been seen in trees. If this was what it appeared to be, the woman and her daughter heard the same two-legged creature in the field at the same time Paul saw it.

Interestingly, Paul's reaction during his brief sighting reflects what we said in the introduction to this book: ...Some people report being completely terrified during their encounter. Others say they feel privileged.

"I felt privileged, and completely at peace," said Paul. "Then again, I never approach cases as though I'm 'chasing' or 'hunting' anything, and neither does Ben (our co-author). We always have an attitude of humility and respect, especially in the woods and fields. I think that makes a difference in the kind of experiences people have."

In fact, Paul always does breathing and mental exercises to put himself in a calm state before undertaking any research and observation in a paranormal case.

Bigfoot Banter?

On the night of Paul's sighting, Shane was at the other end of the 46-acre tract that's believed to be the heart of the Pennsylvania Triangle. In fact, he spent the night in an RV in the woodland clearing where many people have reported seeing Bigfoot, ghostly lights, and experiencing slips in time and space.

"All night long, I heard a low murmuring or chattering outside," reported Shane during one of his frequent appearances on *Behind the Paranormal with Paul & Ben Eno* on WOON 1240 AM in the Boston/Providence area, the weekly radio show we co-host. Shane was clear that he takes the same respectful attitude that we do.

During the same neighborhood meeting in Pennsylvania, Shane related his own experience.

"That's how the Bigfoot talk to each other," commented one man, who had heard the sounds on several occasions.

A Paranormal Pickup?

In an odd sidebar to Shane's night in the woodland clearing, he, at one point late that night, saw a pickup truck drive by, at the near edge of the adjacent cornfield.

"The truck seemed to be red or orange and seemed to have an emblem on the door," Shane recalled. "Sometimes farmers will drive out late at night to check their fields, but not these guys. They got out and were looking in my direction with their flashlights."

This truck passed right by a trail cam Shane had strapped to a tree. When he and Paul checked the cam's photos the next morning, there was no sign of the truck.

Something Big

The morning after Paul's sighting and the apparent Bigfoot chatter overheard by Shane, September 17, both men measured out the area of the upper field, checking for physical evidence.

The grassy field was too dry for tracks, but something large and two-legged had clearly been moving through the tall grass where Paul had seen the creature. It had stopped at the top of the field, then turned back toward the woods, perhaps when the "Shire Theme" ring tonw had come wafting over the field at the prompting of the well-intentioned Ms. Eno.

Shane, who is six feet tall, retraced the walk of whatever it was Paul saw.

"From where I'd been the night before, Shane was clearly one-and-a-half to two-feet shorter than the creature. That made it seven and a half to eight feet tall, at least."

A Thing Between the Trees

On a previous expedition to the Pennsylvania Triangle, in May 2016, Shane had his own Bigfoot encounter – in broad daylight.

"I was in the same clearing where I would sleep in September, when I heard that communication all night," Shane said. "It was raining, and I was sitting in my truck. Suddenly I looked up, and between two trees, about 100 feet away, was what looked like a large, hairy, black creature. At first, I thought it was a bear."

Shane started his engine, and took off across the clearing to get a closer look.

"When I did that, the creature took off to its right, and I could see long arms swinging back and forth. It flushed three deer in the process."

While they have found many other eyewitnesses, and some physical evidence, of Bigfoot in the Pennsylvania Triangle, Paul and Shane are frustrated that, as of this writing, at least, they have been unable to get photos of their encounters, and they realize that this can cause skepticism.

"Even after 47 years of paranormal research, events still tend to happen totally unexpectedly. Even if you have your camera at the ready, it's rare that you can catch something weird as it's happening," Paul pointed out.

Along with Shane, we continue our work in the Pennsylvania Triangle as this book goes to press.

The Big Guy has many names

Known most widely as Bigfoot, the creature (and/or its cousins) is known in North America by many other names. Native Americans refer to Sasquatch. In Florida and other parts of the southern United States, we have the Skunk Ape. Natives of the Pacific Northwest sometimes report the Skookum. The Tsiatko is said to roam the Rocky Mountains. Louisiana is home to the Honey Island Swamp Monster. There's the Wild Man (or Woman) of the Woods, and many other names.

Yeti is a common name for Bigfoot-like creatures from the British Isles to the Pacific coasts of Asia. There are also Almas, the Almasty, the Yeren, the Abominable Snowman and many others. Australians do double-takes when they see the Yowie.

The Patterson-Gimlin Film

When it comes to evidence for the existence of Bigfoot, there are plenty of purported photos, and even some videos. Often considered the quintessential Bigfoot video, and certainly one of the clearest, is the 60-second Patterson-Gimlin Film. It was taken on October 20, 1967, by Roger Patterson and Robert Gimlin, about 25 miles northwest of Orleans, California, from an old

The Monster Hunters

Jeff Hilling

Jeff Hilling describes himself as a Bigfoot historian and researcher. His specialty is the famous Patterson-Gimlin Film of 1967. Jeff appeared on the CBS Radio edition of *Behind the Paranormal with Paul & Ben Eno* on November 22, 2009.

Jeff Hilling

He has studied virtually every available resource on Bigfoot and the Patterson-Gimlin Film, and is the author of the books *The Great Bigfoot Film Mystery, American Bigfoot* and *Bigfoot Booyah.*

Jeff's informative website is devoted exclusively to the subject of the Patterson-Gimlin Film debate.

As Jeff continues his own Bigfoot research, he told us that he has become 80 percent convinced that the Patterson film footage is genuine.

His website: Pattersonfilm.com

logging road adjacent to Bluff Creek, a tributary of the Klamath River.

Many photo and video experts have examined the 8 mm film. Some declare that it's genuine, though others believe that it simply records a man in a Bigfoot costume.

Bigfoot historian and researcher Jeff Hilling appeared on the CBS Radio edition of *Behind the Paranormal* on November 22, 2009, to talk about Bigfoot in general and the Patterson-Gimlin film in particular.

"Bigfoot reports go back to mainstream news articles of the mid-1800s," Jeff told us. "These include strange, hairy beasts, 'wildmen' and creatures from Native American folklore. There's a rich history of sightings, especially here in North America."

What people are actually seeing can be a matter of interpretation, according to Jeff.

"It's interesting to consider that at least some of these reports could actually be 'wildmen' – feral people," he added. "The natives have a rich folklore about Bigfoot. They consider them to be 'elder brothers' of a different tribe, a man or brother in the woods."

Frame 352 of the Patterson-Gimlin Film of 1967 contains the famous "look back" by the apparent Bigfoot. *This frame is in the public domain.*

As evidence of Bigfoot, Jeff considered the Patterson-Gimlin Film significant.

"This is the second most analyzed film of all time, second only to Abraham Zapruder's film of the Kennedy assassination," he pointed out. "It has never been disproved.

"There's no way that Roger Patterson could have foreseen the scrutiny this film would receive, and certainly not the 21st century technology that's been used to scrutinize it. The experts have been taking it apart for over 40 years. If this was a hoax, it's more amazing than an actual Bigfoot."

Nevertheless, there are people who actually claim to have been the man in the Bigfoot suit. But, according to Jeff, their stories don't add up.

"People claim to have been in the suit. Bob Heironimus (of Yakima, Washington) claims he was the man," Jeff said. "But if it was a man in a suit, where's the suit?"

Researchers have made the point that this appears to be a female bigfoot because of its apparent breasts. This would create more work for any costume maker. Nevertheless, Charlotte, North Carolina-based Philip Morris, a costume manufacturer who has provided props for Hollywood films, claimed that he manufactured the costume. Jeff Hilling doubted this.

"If it was a suit, it wasn't Hollywood caliber," Jeff said.

Patterson died in 1971, but he insisted to the end of his life that the film was genuine.

One thing we noticed: In the full version of the film, when Gimlin and the horses approach the alleged Bigfoot, the horses don't seem skittish. That's very unusual, given that Bigfoot has been known to incite panic in farm animals, and total silence even from birds, frogs and insects when it's nearby. So we remain skeptical.

Two Legs or Four?

Jeff suggested that Bigfoot might not always be bipedal. In one of many such encounters, a Utah security guard reported in 2010 that the large-headed Bigfoot he saw was on two legs at first, then dropped to all fours to run away.

"There are many such reports," Jeff said.

The Mystery of Panther Rock

In Anderson County, in north-central Kentucky, the Kentucky Wildman has long been known in a region that we believe is a flap area because of the many kinds of paranormal phenomena reported there. Within this area is Panther Rock, actually a cave on private land. Eyewitness reports have included not only Bigfoot but strange lights and upright canine cryptids. One farmer reported that a 700-pound cow was attacked, and its ears and eyes ripped out.

On May 2, 2011, Philip Spencer (Page 29) appeared on the WOON 1240 edition of *Behind the Paranormal* to tell us about it.

"Panther Rock is a mysteriously alluring place. There are ongoing sightings," Philip said.

"As for the Kentucky Wildman, the term 'wildman' has been used for many years to describe Bigfoot. I think these could sometimes be feral people, but there's a definite Bigfoot connotation," said Philip, who had seen what he believed was the Kentucky Wildman, while watching wildlife at night with a friend.

"It was in Anderson County in 1970. The sighting lasted minutes, and we had a high-powered, car-mounted spotlight on the creature," he assured us. "We watched it walk through a lowland river area, known as a river bottom."

Ben Eno asked how far away the creature was, and how it reacted to the presence of the two men.

"It was about 100 yards or so from us," Philip replied. "We liked to watch animals at night, and it was about two o'clock in the morning. We had the spotlight on a field in that river bottom."

What struck Philip as especially odd was that the field was full of deer.

"When the creature turned to walk away, the deer didn't panic. They themselves just walked away together, all at once. It was the strangest thing to wit-

The Monster Hunters

Philip Spencer

Philip Spencer

Philip Spencer was one of America's quietest and most beloved Bigfoot investigators. A native of Kentucky and author of *The Wildman of Kentucky: The Mystery of Panther Rock*, Philip left us on May 28, 2014, after a battle with heart disease and diabetes. He was 63.

In his May 2, 2011, appearance on the WOON 1240 edition of *Behind the Paranormal with Paul & Ben Eno*, Philip made clear that he was "blessed or cursed with an insatiable curiosity for everything, seeking answers to the mysteries of life, death and the paranormal since childhood." He was active in the Kentucky Bigfoot Research Organization, the American Bigfoot Society, the Tri-State Bigfoot Organization, Pennsylvania Bigfoot Society, and Sasquatch Watch of Virginia.

ness," he said.

"The creature made no sound. It walked until it got to a fence that was three to four feet high. With its size and stride, the creature crossed the fence like it wasn't even there."

Philip emphasized that he and his friend had both grown up in rural Kentucky and were "very experienced outdoor guys. It was natural to us to be in a remote area late at night. But we were frozen. Once it disappeared into the darkness, we just stared at each other for maybe a minute."

The first reports of a Kentucky Wildman come down to us from about 1811, according to Philip.

"Reports have come in consistently over the years, and they became more common as the human population increased. At the same time, I believe the population of Bigfoot has been depleted."

Seeing Bigfoot is a life-milestone, Philip emphasized.

"When you see this creature, it changes you forever. It's like you can't stop wanting to know more."

Philip said he knows the Kentucky Wildman exists.

"I'd just like to know what, specifically, this creature is."

Several years later, in this same area and not 50 yards from the point of his

1970 sighting, Philip encountered Bigfoot again, while walking down an old road.

"I can't say it was the same creature. To me, it was," he told us. "This wasn't the usual encounter, but stunning. Deer came running down off the hillside. A huge doe came bursting across the road right in front of me, then jumped 10 feet down into a field over a bank."

This was the huge field where Philip and his friend had seen the first creature.

"The doe was still running as she hit the river. To my right, up the hill, I could hear the heavy steps of a bipedal creature, thudding on the ground. I tried to see, then I noticed that a huge log had been pushed (down the hillside)."

Paul Eno asked, "Why were those deer frightened, but in the first sighting, a whole herd seemed perfectly calm in the creature's presence?"

"I've asked myself the same question over and over again!" Philip replied. "In 1970, there were about 30 deer within 10 feet of this creature, grazing. Then they just shuffled away."

Philip believed that Bigfoot is omnivorous, eating both meat and vegetation, as do people.

"When deer come into an area in the late fall, you do get more Bigfoot sightings, so I think they do hunt deer."

This is also the area where "Farmer X" recorded what became known as the Frazier Howl, on the Frazier Land, named for a former owner, and which is a paranormal hotspot.

"So many things have occurred on that land," Philip said. "A 20-inch-long Bigfoot track was found there, and strange lights are common."

He noted that Farmer X lives on the tract. He was outside one night when he heard a 'haunting moan' or howl, which he recorded.

"I've had it analyzed, and no one can say what made it," said Philip, who said that the sound prompted some strange responses.

"When animals heard it, they had strong reactions. (Farmer X) has some tough, country farm dogs. They're not afraid of anything. But when they heard the sound, they reacted as though confused."

The Population Question

When Bigfoot researchers join us on *Behind the Paranormal*, we always bring up the question: If Bigfoot is a flesh-and-blood, non-multiversal hominid, how does it stay hidden in areas like the farm country of western Pennsylvania or northern Kentucky, especially since a relatively large number of individuals would be required to maintain a viable breeding population?

"It's been suggested that there are between 500 and 750 of these creatures in North America. I think there are 500 or less," said Philip. "This is a creature that's in its demise. People think Bigfoot is rough and tough, but this is a delicate creature, environmentally sensitive. As humans encroach farther and farther into the wilderness, we are truly bringing this creature to an end."

So, why is there little physical evidence of Bigfoot, and certainly no bodies?

"How often do you see a bear or bobcat carcass, or even see them alive?" Philip asked. "Still, if we're talking about an eight- or nine-foot mammal in the woods, it's a valid question. But what Nature and decomposition can do to a corpse in a short time is stunning."

He pointed out that there are stories of Bigfoot bodies being found over the years, but that they were buried or destroyed before any scientist could see them.

At the same time, Philip agreed that the parallel-world explanation might well account for the dearth of Bigfoot evidence.

"Multiple worlds might very well be real, as theoretical physics suggests. But I try not to use that theory as an excuse or easy way out," Philip stated. "The creature I saw (in 1970) was flesh and blood."

He agreed with us that the Bigfoot walking through the herd of deer might have been invisible to them because of the nature of the parallel-world intersect. The apparent Bigfoot chasing the deer in Philip's other experience might have been fully in our world and, therefore, perceptible to the deer.

"I have no explanation. It makes zero sense," Philip said, "But I'm not one to close doors."

He related another Kentucky case from the same area.

"A man and his son were walking on a rural road. Only about 15 feet in front of them, the creature walks out of a cedar thicket and stops. They froze, and looked at each other. Then the creature walked backwards into the thicket," said Philip.

Needless to say, the man and his son left abruptly.

"The creature they saw had long, matted hair, similar to reports from all over Kentucky. In fact, I think Kentucky will be the state where validity for Bigfoot comes from."

Bigfoot's European Cousins

In 2012, we gave a talk in Woodbridge, England, and visited Rendlesham Forest, the scene of four days of UFO incidents witnessed by U.S. Air Force personnel in December 1980. The affair became known as "Britain's Roswell."

Suspecting that Rendlesham Forest, a 3,700-acre tract located in the Suffolk farm country of eastern England, is actually the center of a paranormal flap area, we did our own research. Not only did we find bizarre occurrences in the area reaching back to Saxon times, we also found that many local people had,

What appear to be an orb and three or more pinpoints of light (the one farthest to the left is red in the original color shot) highlight this photo, taken by the authors in England's infamous Rendlesham Forest on the night of September 21, 2012. At a meeting the next evening, local residents reported encounters with Bigfoot and far more bizarre cryptids in the forest, which the authors believe is the heart of a flap area. On the night this picture was taken, the authors strongly felt they were being followed.

and continue to have, paranormal experiences in the forest. These include Bigfoot, whom the British refer to as the Yeti.

When we visited the forest on September 21 and 22, 2012, in the company of some local radio listeners and an eyewitness to the 1980 UFO incidents, a former U.S. Air Force security policeman, we heard several reports of Yeti sightings there. And we had the overwhelming feeling of being followed as we walked up a forest road to the former East Gate of an old military base.

Researcher Richard Freeman (Page 45) knows all about Bigfoot-like creatures in Britain.

"There are many reports, and I think of the troll legends of mainland Europe, and the Almasty in the Ukraine and Scandinavia," Richard said when he appeared on the CBS Radio broadcast of *Behind the Paranormal* on January 22, 2012.

"Britain is an island, and a few hundred years ago, the forests were thicker. There could very well have been Bigfoot-like creatures."

A Man-Shaped Hole in Reality

Richard shared a very odd report, from Newscastle, in the County of Tyne and Wear, in northeast England.

"A colleague of mine saw a Yeti, but it was black, two-dimensional, and moving fast," Richard said. "It was like a man-shaped hole in reality. This was not a flesh-and-blood animal. It was something stranger."

Weirdness in the Big Thicket

Some of the most striking Bigfoot stories in North America come from the "Big Thicket" area of southeast Texas. Rob Riggs (Page 34) grew up with Bigfoot stories from that area and was a newspaper journalist and publisher in the region for many years. He appeared on *Behind the Paranormal* not long before his death in 2015.

"In 1952, I was seven years old. But I remember newspaper stories about a wildman in the area," Rob recalled. "This was way before Bigfoot was ever even talked about. The term 'Bigfoot' wasn't even used in California until 1958."

This memory stuck with Rob and, 25 years later, when he was a reporter, he decided to see if there had been subsequent sightings.

"I wrote a story in the paper, asking people if they'd had any unusual wildlife

These photos were taken by Rob Riggs and Tom Burnette's trail cam in the mysterious Big Thicket area of Texas in 2009. *Photos courtesy Tom Burnette.*

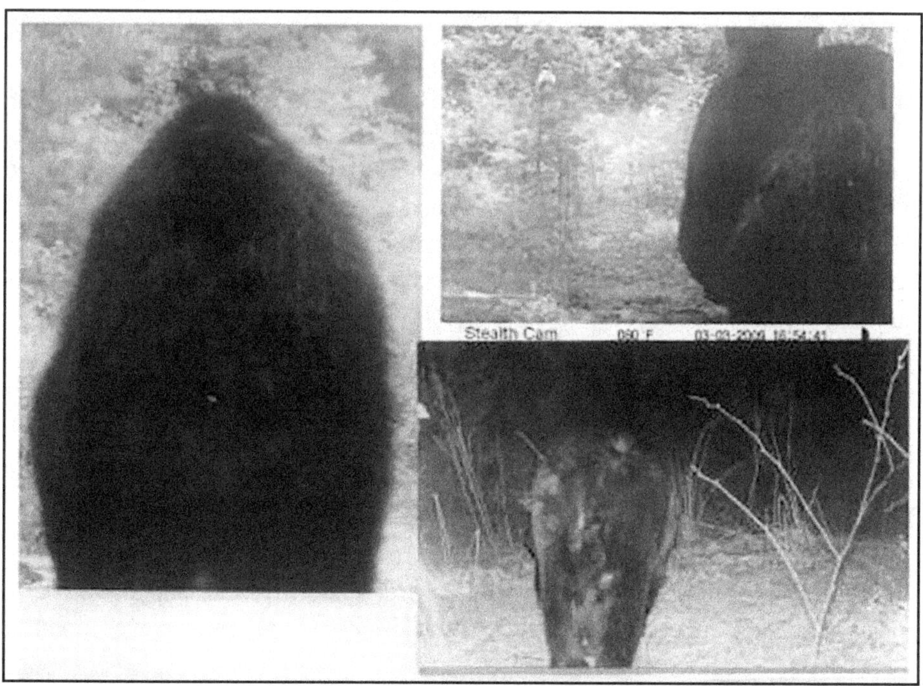

The Monster Hunters
Rob Riggs

Robb Riggs

Rob Riggs, a native of southeast Texas, was a 25-year veteran of newspaper journalism. A respected researcher, author and speaker, Rob passed on November 3, 2015, after a battle with cancer. He was 70.

Rob's books include *In the Big Thicket, Bigfoot: Exploring the Myth & Discovering the Truth*, co-authored with Tom Burnette (page 36) and contributed to *Weird Texas.*

Rob and Tom appeared on the WOON 1240 edition of *Behind the Paranormal with Paul & Ben Eno* on October 27, 2014.

Rob was raised hearing strange stories about things seen in the woods of his native region. He was a featured writer at the annual Texas Book Festival, and he appeared regularly on radio and television.

sightings. I got several immediately. The most convincing was from a couple that had gone out driving, and had their own encounter."

This was reported in the fall of 2003. The couple were driving on the FM (Farm to Market) 1276 Road near the Big Sandy Creek section of the Big Thicket National Preserve. It was after sunset when they saw a two-legged creature run across the road, right in front of them.

"It ran in a bent-over posture, with its arms near or on the pavement sometimes. It ran very quickly and well," one witness was quoted as saying. "The animal was around five feet in height and was covered with long, reddish-brown hair."

The witness's father reported seeing the creature during the same week and in the same location. There was a third sighting report from a woman passer-by a short time later.

Those Orbs Again

"There's another phenomenon in the Big Thicket known as the ghost lights," Rob stated. "Tom Burnette (a North Carolina Bigfoot researcher and experiencer - page 38) and I have concluded that the lights are somehow connected with Bigfoot. We believe that Bigfoot is part of what, in Britain, they call 'Earth Mysteries,' part of a range of phenomena that occur in specific areas due to the presence of aberrant energy fields."

As Rob gathered reports, he ran into people who said they'd seen "apes."

"One couple reported an ape jumping on the hood of their pickup truck in an area where the ghost lights had appeared for at least 100 years. Bigfoot or whatever it was jumped on the hood and was glaring at them menacingly through the windshield."

This happened on Ghost Road, a local lover's lane. The man happened to have a shotgun in the truck.

"He fired at it with both barrels, and all it did was run off into the woods, leaving a big scratch on the hood of their truck," Rob said.

This brought to mind another fun fact about cryptids. They very often seem impervious to weapons. Is this evidence that they really are multiversal creatures, partly in our world and partly in their own?

Back in the Big Thicket, newsman Rob Riggs was beginning to think that Bigfoot sightings were an ongoing phenomenon.

"I got several other stories, and they were very similar to Bigfoot reports from other parts of the country," said Rob, who started doing research on his own and with organizations he trusted in Texas.

"I'm convinced beyond any doubt that there's a version of Bigfoot in the South that runs from East Texas all the way to Virginia, and perhaps as far north as New England. It's much more universal than people realize."

A Deafening Howl

How close had Rob himself been to Bigfoot?

"My closest encounter was when I was alone in the Big Thicket, between Beaumont and my hometown of Sour Lake. One showed up and howled at me from about 50 feet away. It was the most traumatic experience I've ever had in the woods! The sound was so loud that it made the air vibrate! You could feel the vibration in your chest cavity."

Rob described the sound as "overpowering and prolonged."

"There were all kinds of weird undulations and tonal changes. That convinced me beyond any doubt that I was dealing with a real animal."

On the other hand, we wondered, is this more than a "real animal"? Undulations and tonal changes can indicate a language.

"There were other times I've suspected they have been close, but I haven't seen them," Rob continued.

"How did you feel in the presence of this creature?" we asked. "Mildly frightened, terrified, calm, peaceful, curious, threatened, what?"

"Interesting that you ask. I did not feel threatened, and I did not feel terrified," Rob replied. "I felt like I was being acknowledged. I wondered why, because this was in pitch dark. It could have walked right past me and I would never have known it was there. When it was howling, I knew it could take me out if it wanted to."

Rob mentioned physical feelings as well.

"Certainly there's a tingling as in electronic phenomena, and there's often an eerie silence in its presence. All of a sudden everything goes dead quiet. I've seen many reports that talk about that eerie silence."

Since Rob's ear-splitting encounter, two National Park Service rangers had told Rob they heard a similar howl, and "it wasn't from any animal known to live in North America."

We asked Rob if he felt the creature was attempting to communicate with him that night in the Big Thicket.

"That was the feeling I got from it. Bigfoot has extraordinary sensory abilities, as do we. But ours have atrophied with the development of language," Rob replied. "I think Bigfoot is almost what you'd call telepathic. I think it picks up our 'vibes,' so to speak, it picks up our intentionality, even the pictures we have in our heads."

He cited research done in Europe on animal telepathy.

"The conclusion is that telepathy is a common form of communication among animals. We still have it, but we don't use it. Bigfoot has not only not lost it, but has developed it to a very high degree. They're able to use that ability to camouflage themselves; not only to hide but to stalk."

Rob remained open to the multiverse solution, as reflected in the beliefs of indigenous peoples.

"Native Americans talk about Bigfoot's abilities as a shape-shifter. Earth Mysteries include weird lights, weird energy fields, sometimes UFOs. The theory is that aberrant magnetic fields can create portals between parallel worlds. So the natives say that Bigfoot is in two worlds," Rob explained.

"People are talking about parallel worlds, the multiverse, all the time now. It's all theoretically possible. These animals may be native to a closely-parallel reality, and they're able to enter this one under the right conditions, when those portals open."

Rob went a step further.

"We think they might actually be able to facilitate opening the portals. So we're dealing with way more than just an undiscovered animal."

This could explain why so many sightings occur within populated areas. Where else could they hide otherwise but in parallel worlds?

Rob cited the late author and journalist John Keel, who had similar suspicions when he covered the Mothman incidents in the Ohio Valley in the 1960s.

"Keel talked about 'window areas' in connection with various phenomena: Star-like lights moving in the sky, then fireballs as big as the moon, then the ghost lights of basketball size closer to the ground, landed craft, hairy monsters.... The Big Thicket is a window area."

Rob cited the erratic, sometimes bizarre behavior of UFOs and "ghost lights," suggesting that something aside from cryptids might be coming through in window areas.

"You may also have technologies from parallel worlds accessing ours. The behavior of these ghost lights doesn't add up, based on our thermodynamics. We're dealing with things that defy Newtonian physics. It's getting into quantum physics. We may be dealing with macro-quantum events."

Ben noted that some people have trouble accepting the existence of cryptids, perhaps because of the fairy-tale labels we give them.

"I don't like to use the term Bigfoot. I prefer to call it an unknown primate," Rob declared.

"Speaking of window areas, I have two confirmed sightings in the Big Thicket of people seeing spider monkeys in the woods. Spider monkeys are in South America. They can't survive the winters in North America. One report was in the newspaper in the 1960s, and they had a picture of it."

Like us, Rob questioned the assumptions people have about the paranormal in general and cryptids in particular.

"Many people get into Bigfoot research, and they have no idea about the background paved by journalists like John Keel. They start off assuming it's an unknown animal, and they don't even look at the other possibilities."

Bigfoot in the North Carolina Mountains

Tom Burnette (Page 38) of Old Fort, North Carolina, was Rob Riggs's friend, colleague and co-author.

Tom, a real estate investor, lives on property owned by three generations of his family in the Blue Ridge Mountains of western North Carolina. The land adjoins the half-million-acre Pisgah National Forest.

"I inherited over 100 acres next to the forest, and I built my house in the mountains 25 years ago," Tom told us when he appeared on *Behind the Paranormal.*

"I started fixing a property boundary, which was essentially piled-up rocks. I made a lot of noise," Tom said.

Suddenly, he heard running behind him.

"In those days, I carried a gun wherever I went. The running stopped behind a huge oak tree. When I looked, I saw a head that seemed two feet wide. There

The Monster Hunters
Tom Burnette

Tom Burnette

Tom Burnette is a real estate investor who lives in the Blue Ridge Mountains near Old Fort, North Carolina, on land owned by three generations of his family.

Tom's property abuts the half-million acre Pisgah National Forest. This is where Tom has done most of his Bigfoot research, and he has had many hair-rising encounters.

Tom's books include *Bigfoot: Exploring the Myth & Discovering the Truth*, co-authored with Rob Riggs.

Tom appeared with Rob on the WOON 1240 edition of *Behind the Paranormal with Paul & Ben Eno* on October 27, 2014. He has appeared widely in the media.

His website: Tomburnette.blogspot.com

was five to six inches between the eyes, which were solid black. It was just staring at me."

Then it started throwing rocks.

"It was like it wanted me to move. The rocks weren't big enough to hurt me… like it was scraping stuff off the ground and throwing it. It must have thought I was trying to build a structure there."

Tom found the creature's eyes to be striking.

"I could tell there was a tremendous amount of intelligence. Funny: My parents and grandparents had warned me not to build a house in this area, but they wouldn't tell me why."

Growing up, Tom heard their stories about going berry picking, then being run out of the woods "by something big and hairy, and it stank."

This brought up the common belief that Bigfoot has a putrid odor. But this doesn't feature in all reports, and there was no sign of it during the sightings by Paul Eno and Shane Sirois in Pennsylvania, which opened this chapter. We suspect that Bigfoot, or at least some of its variations, has a scent gland that can be used when the creature is alarmed or on the defensive, much like a skunk.

Tom returned to that first experience on his property.

"I wasn't out looking for Bigfoot. It was like being in a science fiction movie!

It was weird."

Tom finally built his house, but farther down the mountain.

"Even then, they peeked in my windows at night. It was scary. I thought they were going to come in and get me. Some nights I lay shaking on the living room floor with my rifle."

We found it interesting that Rob Riggs didn't feel fear in his encounter, but that Tom Burnette did. Eventually, Tom told us, he learned to live with Bigfoot.

"At first, I had a healthy respect," said Tom, who described himself as "an outdoorsman and an educated redneck."

"I did food exchanges with them, and they would pile firewood outside. There are certain areas you can walk through and actually see them behind trees and rocks."

Tom agreed with Rob that Bigfoot has what amounts to a practical mastery of physics, and can traverse world boundaries, or branes, probably at will. Interestingly, Tom lives only a few miles from the famous Brown Mountain Lights, but that's a story for another book.

Much has been made of government secrecy when it comes to UFOs, but are authorities trying to keep a lid on Bigfoot sightings too?

"I've been approached by people I believe are from the government," Tom told us. "They wanted to ask questions."

At one point, Tom said he was approached by a man who said he was with the U.S. Air Force security police.

"I know you write about Bigfoot," Tom reported the man saying. "I have people who guard ICBM silos, and they routinely see seven- to eight-foot-tall beings that appear out of nowhere. We try to photograph them with camera systems inside the missile silos. When my people come out of the silos, they have to see a psychiatrist."

Monsterland

Just before we finished writing this book, Paul Eno accompanied our friends Ronny Le Blanc and Steve Laplume on a hike through an area outside Leominster (pronounced LEMinster), Massachusetts, in an area that's actually, though unofficially, known as Monsterland because of all the odd things seen there over the years.

Ronny (Page 40) is a New England Bigfoot researcher and the author of *Monsterland: Encounters with UFOs, Bigfoot and Orange Orbs.* Steve was an Air Force security policeman at the RAF Bentwaters air base in England during the Rendlesham Forest UFO incidents of 1980, and he sometimes sits in for Ben as co-host of *Behind the Paranormal.* Both men are Leominster natives.

During our hike, in Leominster State Forest on April 22, 2017, we saw some

The Monster Hunters

Ronny LeBlanc

Ronny Le Blanc

Ronny Le Blanc has always been fascinated by all things unexplained. His passions include everything from general paranormal subjects and cryptozoology to alternative history, science and UFOs.

Ronny specializes in the bizarre area known as Monsterland, near his native Leominster, Massachusetts.

The author of *Monsterland: Encounters with UFOs, Bigfoot and Orange Orbs*, Ronny is well-known in the media, having his own podcast, *The Monsterland Podcast*, as well as a show on WAAF 107.3 FM every third Monday, *Monsterland Monday with Matty and Nick.* As we went to press, Ronny was ready to debut his own weekly show on WPKZ 105.3 FM.

He currently works in the marketing and advertising industry in Boston, Massachusetts. Ronny appeared on the WOON 1240 edition of *Behind the Paranormal with Paul & Ben Eno* on April 23, 2017, and again on our live broadcast from the Saucer Symposium in Stratham, New Hampshire, on May 21, 2017.

His website: RonnyLeBlanc.com.

strange, painted markings on trees, and plenty of evidence of coyotes, some of which we stepped in. But there was no sign of Bigfoot, despite the frequency of sightings in Monsterland.

The next day, Ben was away, celebrating his first wedding anniversary, and Paul, Steve and Ronny did the *Behind the Paranormal* radio show.

"Bigfoot is often thought of as a West Coast phenomenon," Steve noted. "When did it migrate to the East Coast?"

"We often think of Bigfoot being in northern California, Oregon and Washington. But people are having experiences and sightings all over the country," Ronny replied.

One of the first reports Ronny heard from Monsterland came from a couple who were hiking in the same area we had explored the day before the show.

"They found a series of barefoot prints, with a six-foot stride between each print, and in a straight line. They felt as though they were being watched the

Above is the spot on Old Mill Road in Leominster, Massachusetts, where an unfortunate motorist is said to have had a traumatic, perhaps fatal, Bigfoot encounter in the late 1950s. This tunnel is considered an entrance to Monsterland. Below, the tunnel is seen from the Monsterland side. *Photos courtesy Ronny Le Blanc*

whole time," Ronny stated.

He went to the site to assist in making plaster casts of the footprints, and this led to his appearance on the Animal Planet television show *Finding Bigfoot*. The show unleashed a slew of reports from local people who had been silent for fear of ridicule.

"Monsterland is a small area of southern Leominster, near the border of the Town of Lancaster. It got its name because kids would go there to party or ride dirt bikes or ATVs, and they'd have encounters. Things would be thrown at them, they'd hear strange noises, and sometime see a creature," Ronny said.

Monsterland is bounded by Old Mill Road and the oddly-named Jungle Road. While stories of creature sightings in the area go back to 1884, according to Ronny, the name Monsterland apparently took root in the late 1950s. The story is that a man was driving on Old Mill Road, near an old stone bridge, and saw a Bigfoot-like creature by the side of the road.

"The man ran into a nearby bar and told the manager what he'd seen. He was frantic," said Ronny.

The man finally got the bar manager to call the police, then vowed to return to the scene.

"He headed back to the spot, and Leominster police showed up at the bar minutes after he left. Officers proceeded to the scene of the sighting. They found the man's car, with the door open, the lights on and the engine running. The man was never found."

While the police record contains no missing-person report from that period that matches this account, the story was enough to jump-start the legends.

Ronny Le Blanc, left, explores Leominster State Forest with sometime* Behind the Paranormal *guest co-host Steve Laplume on April 22, 2017. Paul Eno took the photo.

There have, however, been plenty of credible Bigfoot sightings by hikers, hunters and others during the ensuing years.

"One farmer saw a creature on two legs snag some of his pigs and run off," said Ronny, who sees a clear connection between Bigfoot and sightings of strange lights.

"Before this was known as Monsterland, it was actually known as the UFO Landing Area," he said. "People would see craft hovering over power lines, supposedly there was a craft that actually landed, and there were marks on the ground from landing gear."

There's a long history of "orange orbs" in Monsterland, including sightings at nearby Fort Devens, one of the largest military bases in New England until 1996, and still home to a busy Army Reserve training area and a military intelligence school.

"I found an old letter from 1952 reporting that eight orange balls of light flew over the base, and they had no idea what these things were," Ronny recalled.

"I've had numerous experiences with these balls of light, and so have many other people. And I believe they're associated with Bigfoot. In fact, the more I've gotten into this, the more things that have happened to me, almost like John Keel!"

The Woonsocket Wild Man?

"As a teenager, things are confusing enough, but even more so if a cryptid is involved," Ben Eno said as he recalled a frightening Bigfoot incident in the woods of northern Rhode Island in 2008, almost on his own doorstep.

It was the first year of the *Behind the Paranormal* radio show, but Ben's parents insisted that he have the experience of a standard job as well.

"I was 16 and working in the kitchen of a nursing home/hospice facility. It was a normal teenage job," Ben said.

This facility was located at the top of the heavily wooded Fairmount Hill, just above the Eno homestead, on the Woonsocket/North Smithfield town line.

"We've mentioned this hill on our show a couple of times. It's a weird place. In the past it's been a UFO hotspot, the location of the old New England legend of the Devil's Hole, and the kids tell legends of ghosts and creatures in the woods," Ben said.

"There was an unspoken rule among the neighborhood kids when I was growing up: Never go into the woods at night. As a dumb teenager, thinking myself invincible, not much scared me. I'll admit that I've had some weird experiences in there, but none quite like this."

That year, Ben regularly walked up the hill, through the woods, to get to work.

"On this particular spring day, it was raining just enough to be a nuisance, but

An artists's conception of the Yeti of the Himalayas. RikoBest/Shutterstock

I still preferred to walk because I enjoyed the forest so much. The days were getting longer, so my boldness for walking home grew," he continued.

"It was a little after 8 o'clock when I left work through the back door. The path for home was only a stone's throw away."

The sun was setting, and dusk was approaching. The unspoken rule tugged at the back of Ben's mind, and he felt a sudden urge to stay away from the woods.

"During the day, the woods of Fairmount Hill are peaceful and beautiful, but in the waning hours of the day, they seem more sinister and foreboding."

As he descended the darkening path through the trees, Ben suddenly felt that he was being watched.

"I was afraid. I turned my head to the right, and about 25 feet away, behind a large boulder, I saw an almost cone-shaped head rise up. It was hairy, very hairy, and I remember the eyes being a bright red as it made eye contact with me."

Ben stood there in shock. He'd been working with his dad in paranormal research for over two years, but he wasn't ready for this.

"I was used to ghosts at this point but, whatever this was...to this day I'm not entirely sure what it was," he recalled.

"If it was Bigfoot, there was no stereotypical smell. My decision was to get home as quickly as possible. I slipped and slid all the way down the freshly rained-on path, but I made it home to safety."

The Monster Hunters

Richard Freeman

Richard Freeman

Richard Freeman is an adventurer and trained zoologist specializing in cryptids, which he travels all over the world to investigate. He's also an author, zoological journalist, and media personality.

Zoological director of the U.K.-based Centre for Fortean Zoology (CFZ), Richard co-edits both the journal, *Animals & Men* and the annual *CFZ Yearbook.*

Richard has authored or co-authored a number of books, and has contributed to Fortean and zoological magazines, newspapers and periodicals around the world. He lectures widely.

Richard appeared on the CBS Radio edition of *Behind the Paranormal* on January 22, 2012.

Richard first developed his passion for cryptozoology in the 1970s by watching *Dr. Who*. His interest in the unexplained and zoology grew in tandem. He became a zookeeper at Twycross Zoo in Leicestershire, working with more than 400 exotic species "from ants to elephants, but with a special interest in crocodilians."

His website: Cfz.org.uk/

The Nasty Almasty

Globetrotting cryptozoologist Richard Freeman is convinced that he and a colleague came very close to an encounter with the Almasty, a Russian version of Bigfoot, in the Caucusus mountains in 2008.

"It was 2:30 in morning, and we were at old farmhouse," Richard told us when he appeared on *Behind the Paranormal.*

"The house had an L-shaped veranda. Suddenly we heard a deep, guttural vocalization. Something was moving with two legs on that veranda. We ran toward it with our cameras, but it had disappeared into the night."

With a height of five to six feet, very human looking and slightly ape-like, the Almasty is similar to the Yeti, but has shorter arms, according to Richard.

"He has less hair (black or brown, as does the Yeti) on the face and body than the other hominids. It feeds on berries. Sometimes it attacks sheep, but it eats only their livers," he explained.

"Being a nocturnal creature, it's very difficult to catch a glimpse of this elusive hominid," Richard added. "In some cases, people have attempted to shoot the creature. These individuals reportedly died afterwards under mysterious circumstances."

What is Bigfoot?

Finally, we come to the question, and there are almost as many answers as there are experiencers. Shape-shifter, multiversal creature, flesh-and-blood mammal, alien being, dumb animal or brilliant physicist, or survival of the supposedly extinct (but proven to have existed) Gigantopithecus? Civilized or not, friend or foe? All of the above or none of the above?

It sometimes seems that the more research we do, the further we get from an answer.

"Soviet scientists speculated that the Chuchunaa, or the Siberian Snow Man, represents the last surviving remnant of the Siberian paleo-asiatic aborigines who retreated to the upper reaches of the Yana and Indigirka rivers," Richard told us.

"Aboriginal people believe they come from different worlds or are shape-shifters. I believe the vast majority are flesh-and-blood animals," he continued.

"We have the false notion that the world has been mapped and explored. It has not been. That's true for South America, Africa, Asia, even part of North America. There are parts of the world where you can travel for 1,000 miles and not see another human."

Paul asked: "Some people believe that Bigfoot and its cousins are intelligent, even benevolent. What say you?"

"Certainly intelligent," Richard replied. "You do hear stories of them saving drowning people, etc. Animals do sometimes help each other."

In the words of researcher Albert Rosales (page 100), "Bigfoot is definitely an intelligent being that has powers far beyond what we're used to, and that are perhaps interdimensional. I don't think we'll catch one."

2 MOTHMAN

As heard on

Achieve Radio, August 17, 2008, October 12, 2008
WOON 1240 AM, October 18, 2009, April 10, 2016, December 4, 2016
CBS Radio May 1, 2011, August 25, 2013

One of the oddest paranormal incidents in American history began, according to most researchers, in November 1966.

Regardless of the date, "many people don't realize that this area was a hotbed for UFO activity also. Some people saw Mothman, giant birds and the other phenomena as somehow connected with this UFO activity," said researcher Jeff Wamsley (Page 50) when he appeared on *Behind the Paranormal with Paul & Ben Eno* on October 5, 2008

"This area" is the Ohio River Valley in West Virginia and Ohio, and the center of this paranormal activity was (some say *is*) the area around Point Pleasant, West Virginia. As a 13-year-old boy at his childhood home in Connecticut in 1966, Paul Eno remembers his mother showing him articles in the *Hartford Courant* about a "giant bird" being seen in West Virginia.

Jeff filled in the story.

"About three miles north of Point Pleasant is the 'TNT Area.' (Today it's the McClintic Wildlife Management Area.) During World War II, it was the site of an ammunition factory. After the war, it was a place for kids to run around and drag race."

It was the dark and non-stormy night of November 15, 1966. Being a Tuesday, it seems an odd night for two recently married young couples to be out at the TNT Area. In the car were Steve and Mary Mallette, along with Roger and Linda Scarberry.

One of the most common conceptions of Mothman, as depicted by artist Karin Mansberg.

The Mothman statue in Point Pleasant is generally considered to be one of the most accurate likenesses of the creature as described by eyewitnesses.
Photo courtesy Jeff Wamsley/Mothman Museum

"They were…up there drag racing. About 11 p.m., they were driving past what was called the North Power Plant, a building three stories tall, with a smokestack. At the time, it was vacant," Jeff explained.

"As they drove around a turn, they spotted what they thought was a man in the middle of the road."

According to the description of one of the young women, Linda Scarberry, "it was about seven feet tall. It had wings that were visible on its back. The tips of the wings could be seen above its shoulders."

Its body was like that of a "slender, muscular man," Linda told interviewer Donnie Sargent Jr., as recorded in the book *Mothman: The Facts Behind the Legend,* co-authored with Jeff.

The creature's body was "flesh colored," Linda added. "Its wings were an ashen white…. The wings looked like angel wings. Its face couldn't be seen because the eyes simply hypnotized you when you looked into them."

The creature made no sound, according to Linda. And the scenario got weirder.

"When we first saw it, we had just topped a hill in the TNT area, and when the headlights of our car hit it, it looked directly at us, as if it was scared," she continued.

The young people were astounded to see that the creature had a wing caught in a guy wire by the side of the road near the North Power Plant.

"It was pulling on its wing with its hands, trying to free itself. Its hands were really big. It was really scared."

The creature, or one of the creatures, the media would soon dub "Mothman" seemed just as afraid of the young people as they were of it.

"We were all screaming," Linda told Donnie. "But we couldn't perform the actual action of leaving the scene. It was like we were hypnotized."

The creature finally freed its wing, then *ran* into the power plant building.

"I felt sorry for it…. We thought it might have been some sort of machine or something, possibly being controlled by the UFOs or whatever was in them."

The Monster Hunters

Jeff Wamsley

Jeff Wamsley was born and raised in Point Pleasant, West Virginia. He was neighbors with original Mothman witnesses Linda and Roger Scarberry in 1966, and was six years old when the Silver Bridge collapsed in 1967.

Jeff Wamsley

Jeff gained more interest in the Mothman story after picking up a copy of John Keel's book, *The Mothman Prophecies*, while in junior high school, and he recognized many of the names.

Jeff has written two books on the subject: *Mothman: The Facts Behind The Legend* (co-authored with Donnie Sargent Jr. in 2001), and *Mothman: Behind the Red Eyes* (2005).

He opened the world's only Mothman Museum in 2006 and was a co-founder of the annual Mothman Festival in 2003. Jeff has appeared on numerous televison shows, including *Unsolved Mysteries*, *MonsterQuest*, *Mysteries at the Museum* and many others.

Jeff currently teaches graphic design at the Mason County Career Center and holds a bachelor's degree in art-design and a master's degree in adult education.

He appeared on one of the earliest broadcasts of *Behind the Paranormal with Paul & Ben Eno* on October 5, 2008, on Phoenix-based Achieve Radio.

His website: Mothmanlives.com.

As soon as the creature disappeared, the trance-like atmosphere dissipated, and the young people high-tailed it back toward Point Pleasant. But it was far from the end of their terrifying night, because Mothman followed them.

"We saw it sitting in different places as we drove back down Route 62 toward Point Pleasant, and we saw it sitting in various places once we got into town," Linda said.

When the young people first left the TNT Area, they were startled to see the creature sitting atop a billboard by the side of the road. When the car headlights caught it, the creature quickly rose straight up into the air, according to Linda.

"That's when it followed us and hit the top of the car two or three times while

The Monster Hunters

Susan Sheppard

Susan Sheppard

Susan grew up just a few hills away from the first Mothman sighting. A celebrated psychic medium and a descendant of local Native Americans, her interest in the unexplained stems from her paranormal experiences during the Mothman period.

A native of Parkersburg, West Virginia, Susan has assisted local police in missing-person cases. An award-winning author, artist and poet, she has written a number of books and articles, and she has appeared on radio and television. Susan has worked as a psychic medium since age 14 and as a paranormal investigator for the last decade.

She has made a number of appearances on *Behind the Paranormal with Paul & Ben Eno.*

Her website: Parkersburgtours.com

we were going over 100 miles per hour down Route 62...." Linda said.

At one point, they saw a dead German shepherd by the side of the road. And they saw the creature itself as it crouched atop a flood wall by the Ohio River. According to Linda, its arms were around its knees, and its wings were folded against its back.

The two couples barrelled into the Mason County Sheriff's Office and ran right into Deputy Millard Halstead. Needless to say, the officers were skeptical, but thought twice when they saw how terrified the Malettes and Scarberrys were, and realized they hadn't been using alcohol or drugs. As for the police, they didn't see the creature, at least not that night, but officers reported "shadows" circling the North Power Plant. Later on, Halstead and other officers reported loud, howl-like sounds and strange electrical disturbances on their radios in the TNT vicinity. During daylight, odd tracks were found there. Over the course of this Mothman episode, several officers reported sightings of their own.

It wasn't long before people all over the area were seeing the Mothman.

On November 24, for example, a family of four were driving past the TNT Area when they saw "a giant flying creature with red eyes."

In *The Mothman Prophecies*, author John Keel reported that cars, full of men "bristling with guns," were soon circling the TNT area, looking for the creature. Hundreds of curiosity-seekers, along with television and radio crews from all over the country, descended on Point Pleasant, mobbing the TNT Area at night.

According to Keel, however, Mothman had no intention of being outsmarted.

"He staged his appearances with clever showmanship, popping up in unexpected places in front of witnesses who had previously been skeptical."

Jeff Wamsley told us about the big-bird theory.

"They brought in professors from West Virginia University, and they said that all it was was a sandhill crane," Jeff said during his radio interview. "Witnesses I talked to literally laughed at that. They said it was much larger, the size of a man."

Jeff, who owns and operates the Mothman Museum in Point Pleasant and organizes the annual Mothman Festival each September, had actually interviewed someone who worked with sandhill cranes at a reserve in the Midwest.

"She said that sandhill cranes are inquisitive, and will walk right up to people and cars. But as far as the build or body of this creature is concerned, these birds just didn't fit the description."

Mothman sightings around Point Pleasant went on for a year and a half.

"Some people believe that Mothman never left," said Jeff. "A lot of the original witnesses won't talk, but there are some who will. And the sightings today aren't nearly as heavy as they were back in the '60s."

Footsteps on the Roof

Paul Eno spoke at the West Virginia Paranormal Conference, held in Parkersburg, West Virginia, not far from Point Pleasant, in 2003. Ben Eno hadn't yet joined his dad's paranormal adventures, but he attended the conference and remembers meeting one of the original eyewitnesses.

"Several people told us about their Mothman experiences," said Ben, singling out conference organizer Susan Sheppard (Page 51), a paranormal researcher and author who lives in Parkersburg.

"Susan was a little girl in 1966, and she remembers hearing footsteps on their roof during the Mothman episode," Ben added.

Other witnesses reported red eyes peeping through their windows or out from under furniture, poltergeist activity in their homes, strange people around town (such as the "men in black" or MIBs), and even heightened psychic abilities.

"A man named Newell Partridge from Doddridge County, whose kids went to school with Susan Sheppard, owned a German shepherd named Bandit. The dog disappeared after they saw red lights in their field," Jeff noted.

It's possible that the dog's body the Mallettes and Scarberrys saw by the roadside that first night was Bandit's, but it would have had to travel 80 miles in a few hours.

"The next night, Marcella Bennett and her brother, Raymond Wamsley, were bringing her three-year-old-daughter to visit relatives who lived near the TNT Area," Jeff continued. "Marcella Bennett went to her car, and the thing was standing there, looking at her. She said it had a light tan look."

Terrified, Marcella ran back to the house.

"It followed her, came up onto the porch and peered in the windows. This was witnessed by family members," said Jeff. "Marcella was one of the few people who came face-to-face with Mothman," said Jeff. "To this day, she won't drive at night."

The strange "Men in Black" (MIBs) figured prominently in the Mothman affair. There's even an exhibit dedicated to them at the Mothman Museum in Point Pleasant.

Photo courtesy Jeff Wamsley/Mothman Museum

Sightings into the 1990s

Occasional Mothman sightings were reported in the TNT Area into the early 1990s, Jeff told us, adding that the advent of reality television hasn't made verifying reports any easier.

"There are so many TV shows and books on the subject, and so many people want to make documentaries in the area, that you have to be wary. People today want to get on TV."

That wasn't the case in the 1960s, however.

"In the '60s, people didn't want the notoriety," Jeff said. "Many surviving witnesses refuse to be interviewed to this day. Those who agree to talk have described (Mothman) to me as something they'd never seen before, even in a horror movie."

It's difficult to exaggerate the fear that Mothman sightings created throughout the region.

"There was tremendous terror," Jeff said. "Elementary schools wouldn't let children go outside for recess. If people were seeing a giant bird, school authorities reasoned that it could swoop down and pick a kid up."

It wasn't just three or four witnesses, either. There were over 100 reported sightings in 1966 and 1967.

"If this was a hoax, someone would have come forward by now," Jeff stated. "And it wasn't just young couples seeing this, but prominent business people who really put their reputations on the line by coming forward."

What is Mothman?

At that point, Ben asked the simple question: "What is Mothman?"

Jeff paused. "Witnesses can't pinpoint it. Theories have included a mutated bird because of all the chemicals at the TNT site. In the 1980s, it was an EPA Superfund clean-up site."

Whatever Mothman might be, the entire scenario is the stuff of which science fiction movies are made. Jeff mentioned another theory.

"Others thought this was some kind of military experiment, with someone in a suit, maybe using a jetpack. I've heard it all!"

New York journalist John Keel investigated the happenings on-scene while they were taking place, and eventually wrote the book *The Mothman Prophecies.* He believed that the multiverse, or "window area" explanation was the most logical.

"It's true that where you have one type of phenomenon, you're probably going to find other types as well," cryptid researcher Linda Godfrey (page 71) said when we interviewed her. "John Keel talked about window areas. In the case of the Mothman events, they also saw UFOs and MIBs. Keel also had weird electronic things going wrong with his own telephone in New York."

Jeff Wamsley made it clear that the window-area or multiverse idea has merit.

"The Mothman events were accompanied by a flap (of other paranormal phenomena)."

He also cited some physical evidence.

"They did find strange footprints, especially in the TNT area."

The media broke the Mothman story in the person of Mary Hyre, the Point Pleasant correspondent for the *Athens* (Ohio) *Messenger.*

"She broke the story, and John Keel joined forces with her," Jeff said. "She was visited by MIBs, and they weren't happy with her causing what they called a panic."

MIB Mischief

Some of the witnesses also had visits from these bizarre characters.

"People reported that the MIBs would act irrationally, and that they had a pale, Oriental complexion. And they never presented any identification," Jeff said.

"John Keel reported that some of his cameras and film were missing."

Military veterans said that men wearing Air Force uniforms would show up at their doors, but wore the uniforms and insignia incorrectly.

"Newell Partridge said that, after the red lights appeared and the dog went missing, an Air Force officer came to his house with another guy, asking questions," Jeff told us.

"Keel was back and forth to New York, and he reported some odd problems with his telephone. There were strange noises, and strange people at the other end. He felt that the phone was tapped."

Jeff speculated that at least some of the MIBs in the Point Pleasant area could have been curiosity-seekers made up to look like Air Force officers, a federal crime, just to get first-hand stories. But sometimes the MIBs would ask to keep everyday objects, such as pens and ashtrays, then walk away as if they'd acquired a valuable antique.

"They'd stare at a pencil like they'd never seen anything like it," Jeff stated. "Strange people would approach Mary Hyre when she was in her newspaper office. They'd ask for people or addresses that didn't exist. One went into the Mason County Courthouse and asked for someone the staff had never heard of. And these MIBs never blinked their eyes."

According to Keel, Mary Hyre put up with all sorts of electronic mischief as well.

"My phones have gone crazy, even my unlisted numbers," he quoted her as saying. "Strangers call me at all hours of the day and night. Sometimes I get funny beeping sounds."

Jeff said that he'd spoken with a witness a few days before our radio interview.

"One guy walked into their house and just rummaged through papers. He was dressed in black, with an overcoat. He was spooked and took off when he saw that she was home.

"Another woman reported a visit by two MIBs in black turtleneck sweaters, and it was 95 degrees outside. When they left, they didn't get into a car. They walked over a hill."

There might be plenty of undiscovered witnesses to the Mothman phenomenon, according to Jeff.

"Visitors to the Mothman Museum sometimes turn out to be undiscovered witnesses from around the world," he said.

During the show, a listener from California asked if Mothman could be UFO-related because both phenomena were seen in the area at the same time. It's certainly possible, but no-one really knows.

Treated for Shock

Jeff told us about still other eyewitnesses.

"Two nurses were on duty at the Pleasant Valley Hospital in Point Pleasant. They told me they were on duty one night when two women were brought in

The authors visit the Mothman Museum in Point Pleasant in 2007.

and had to be treated for shock. They had definitely seen something and had to be sedated."

These nurses approached Jeff to tell their stories.

Collapse of the Silver Bridge

The Mothman Prophecies film, released in 2002 and bearing a vague resemblance to John Keel's book of that name, makes a connection between Mothman's appearance and the December 15, 1967, collapse of the Silver Bridge, which actually crossed the Ohio River between Henderson, West Virginia, just south of Point Pleasant, and Gallipolis, Ohio. On that pre-Christmas evening, traffic on the bridge was bumper-to-bumper.

"Was there a connection with the Silver Bridge collapse?" Jeff asked the rhetorical question. "It was caused by failed eye bolt #13, which snapped. After the collapse, the entire Mothman affair died down. Maybe people's attention was diverted because of the disaster. The movie connects it, but I doubt it."

The Mothman Museum actually has some props from the movie, along with many original artifacts, such as hand-written police reports about the phenomena.

Other Explanations for Mothman

Those who accept the multiverse explanation for cryptids might suggest that Mothman, or the Mothmen, could have been inter-world tourists. Or, given the fear reportedly shown by the creature during its initial encounter with the young people, perhaps it stumbled into our world unintentionally.

Could there have been a military explanation for Mothman, or at least a military connection? Some of our subsequent radio guests were open to that idea. In fact, as we've mentioned elsewhere, we have solid information that the military, or some group that looks like the military, is studying flap areas in order to, in effect, weaponize the paranormal, appearing to be able to manipulate time and space, and perhaps even control or use the inhabitants of parallel realities.

In any case, Mary Hyre, the local reporter, died four years after the collapse of the Silver Bridge.

"Her niece confirmed to me that Mary was scared because of the MIBs," Jeff said.

Did the MIBs stop harassing people after the bridge collapsed?

"Yes and no," Jeff declared. "There were reports of them walking on the bridge before the collapse. That might have diverted attention from the Mothman. I think there was still Mothman activity, but it didn't get as much limelight."

Jeff acknowledged the occurrence of collateral phenomena, as in a typical paranormal flap area.

"There were ghostly occurrences and, of course, the UFOs. John Keel claimed that lights flashed at UFOs were replied to. UFOs were seen in broad daylight, several times from the street in Point Pleasant that I grew up on. Linda Scarberry and her husband lived on the same street."

Jeff's Interpretation

"I'm still searching," Jeff said. "Was it a large bird, a physical creature? I suspect that there could be a UFO connection. It's been 42 years as of this show, and I'm still trying to get interviews with some of the witnesses."

Jeff made the point that Mothman isn't just an Ohio Valley phenomenon. He, she or it has been and is seen around the globe.

"Many of the descriptions from around the world fit the descriptions of what was seen in and around Point Pleasant. But it's all hard to validate.

Who's on First?

Susan Sheppard gave us some other Mothman stories in one of her many appearances on *Behind the Paranormal.*

"Most people believe the first Mothman encounter was the seven-foot-tall,

The Monster Hunters

Robin Bellamy

Robin Pyatt Bellamy

Robin was born in Point Pleasant, West Virginia in the early 1960's and lived for many years in nearby Ravenswood. The child of a Republican Dad and a Democrat Mom, Robin learned early that there are many sides to every issue. She approaches her research in the same way.

As a child, Robin's mother brought her along on extensive research trips to dig up the family history. She now maintains extensive genealogical projects.

Married with three children, Robin found herself living in Toronto, Canada, in 2000. Through a series of unusual events, she became a member of Toronto Ghosts and Hauntings Research Society and added paranormal research to her resumé. Robin has served that organization as a director and its parent organization, PSICAN (Paranormal Studies and Investigations Canada), as a board member. She recently became director of cryptozoology.

Robin is the author of *Haunt Cuisine*, a collection of recipes and attendant ghost stories from North America, and *Haunted Hospitality*, the historical account of the ghosts of the Lowe Hotel in Point Pleasant.

Her website: Robinbellamy.com

humanoid creature first sighted by Roger and Linda Scarberry and their friends on November 15. It had a wingspan of eight to 12 feet and was seen on a country road outside Point Pleasant," Susan told us.

"In fact, the previous night, in Center Point, about 80 miles away, in Doddridge County, a farmer named Newell Partridge saw red eyes in his barn. I remember my sister coming home and saying that Paula Partridge just saw these same red eyes in the barn."

Susan corroborated the stories about Bandit the German shepherd, the UFO sightings and the MIBs. Then she told us about bizarre happenings at her own home.

A Strange, High-Pitched Wailing

"I was a small girl during the Mothman occurrences," said Susan. "I heard footsteps on our roof, like someone had dropped out of a helicopter. It was between two and three in the morning."

Whatever it was would walk around for 10 or 15 minutes, then leave, according to Susan. Meanwhile, Susan and her family lived near the Partridges, and they heard the following story right from them. It was the night of November 14, 1966.

"Newell Partridge and his son, Roger, were watching TV at about 10:30 p.m., when the TV suddenly went off. Then a strange, high-pitched wailing or screaming came out of the TV," Susan stated, making the point that the event wasn't unlike some of the electrical phenomena portrayed in *The Mothman Prophecies* film.

"People had headaches, and then Bandit the dog began barking in a very atypical way. With their flashlights, Newell and Roger could see Bandit barking at something in the barn, which was roughly a football-field's length away," said Susan.

"By the time they got to the barn, a feeling of dread overcame them. Bandit snarled, then went into the barn. Newell and Roger could see red eyes or orbs. To them, they seemed like red electric lights."

To their horror, the two men watched as a huge figure in the barn's dark interior lumbered up from a sitting or crouching position.

"They were terrified, and they ran back to the house. The TV came back on, and Bandit stopped barking," Susan recalled.

The dog never came to the porch for his breakfast the next morning.

"Mary Partridge saw no trace of the dog, except paw prints that went around in a circle. Then they stopped, as if Bandit had been lifted up."

The dog was never seen again. Could it have been Bandit's body the Malettes and Scarberrys saw along the road during their harrowing experience the night after the Partridges' incident? If so, the dog somehow traveled some 80 miles in a few hours, as Jeff Wamsley noted previously.

Mary found prints in the dirt floor of the barn that looked like huge turkey tracks. According to Susan, the famous Mothman statue in downtown Point Pleasant represents a creature that would have been far too small to produce those tracks. The Partridges connected the entire experience with Mothman when they read the newspaper account of the young couples' experience at the TNT Area.

"In the following months, Mothman was seen all over West Virginia and in southern Ohio," Susan said. "Many of the witnesses were very credible people, not the type to tell stories."

Susan agreed with Jeff Wamsley that the sandhill crane theory was ridiculous.

"It was a supposedly scientific explanation for something there's no other explanation for," she commented.

Susan expanded on the young people's experience on the night of November 16, which amounted to a car chase, with Mothman doing the chasing.

"The thing was right over their car, flying with them. Its wings were beating, hitting the car doors on both sides. When the police checked the car, they found the doors on both sides scratched."

In fact, Linda Scarberry claimed that the creature followed them home to 30th Street in Point Pleasant.

"Linda said the thing was outside their window all night," Susan stated, adding that, for the rest of her life, Linda would never look out the window after dark.

Over the next week, Mothman became big news in the local press. People would see the creature in their yards. A woman in the state capital, Charleston, some 55 miles from Point Pleasant, saw it one day when she went out to get her newspaper.

Evidently, the name Mothman was coined by some anonymous Associated Press reporter or editor when the wire service picked up the story.

"The name Mothman was a media creation, after a cartoon character in the Batman comics. Superheroes were very popular in the '60s," Susan said.

The Coming of Indrid Cold

Then there was the matter of Indrid Cold, who features prominently in *The Mothman Prophecies* film. In fact, Indrid was one of the first characters to turn up as the Mothman drama unfolded. He or it was a strange, but nevertheless human-looking, figure who, according to salesman Woodrow "Woody" Durenberger, emerged from a landed UFO and claimed to be from the planet Lanulos.

This occurred at about 7 p.m. on November 2, 1966, on a road near Parkersburg, West Virginia, up the river from Point Pleasant, before Mothman made his official appearance at the TNT area.

"Woody described the spaceship as about 35 feet across. An ordinary-looking man stepped out, wearing a long, black trench coat," Susan said.

Indrid looked about 35 years of age and was about six feet tall. According to Woody, when Indrid spoke, his lips never moved. Taunia Durenberger Bowman, Woody's daughter, has been a guest on *Behind the Paranormal* several times. She verified that Indrid Cold – whatever or whoever he was – existed and even visited their home in Mineral Wells, West Virginia.

The saga of Indrid and Woody, who reportedly developed a friendship, punc-

Mothman is far from forgotten in Point Pleasant. The Mothman Museum (above), operated by Jeff Wamsley, welcomes thousands of visitors annually. There's even an annual Mothman Festival (below) that grows each year. Photos courtesy Jeff Wamsley/The Mothman Museum

tuates an already bizarre period in the Ohio Valley. Susan didn't believe that the Indrid Cold affair and Mothman were connected.

A flap in more ways than one?

Mothman flapping along after cars is one thing. But Susan agreed with us on the multiverse idea – that the entire region was, and probably still is, a paranormal flap area. That's especially true given the multitude of phenomena taking place during the same period.

"I believe it's more interdimensional. We had the UFOs, the MIBs, not to mention Indrid Cold," Susan said. "We had poltergeist activity at our house. The TV did the whining and wailing, and the Partridges had poltergeist activity, too."

An eyewitness appears on our show

Today, Robin Bellamy (Page 58) is a Canadian paranormal researcher and author, but she grew up in Point Pleasant. As a child, she and her family saw Mothman with their own eyes – in broad daylight.

"We were driving south along the Ohio River, just south of Ravenswood, West Virginia, parallel to some railroad tracks," Robin told us. "I thought it was a deep-sea diver! It was standing between the tracks and the river. We drove by, and he was just standing there, and it was in the daytime. So I have a pretty good idea what he looked like."

The creature's height was "a little overwhelming – seven to eight feet," according to Robin, who believes there was more than one Mothman in the area.

"There would have to be about 500 to sustain a breeding population, but that assumes this is an actual, biological creature. I believe it is biological, while some believe it's interdimensional, others that it's alien, and still others that it's some kind of ghostly manifestation."

"Perhaps it's all of the above," Paul suggested.

Robin said that the answer to what Mothman is will depend on whom you ask. She noted that "the idea of Mothman has been around forever."

"Even in ancient times, there were hieroglyphs of beings that were half-man, half bird. And there were concepts of creatures like the Pheonix and the Thunderbird. In the Orient, they're usually flying women. In Portugal, Britain and other areas, they're bird people," Robin explained.

"There was a 13-month period in the 1960s where hundreds of people in a small town saw this thing. It was a birdman, for lack of a better term, with the body of a man and the wings of a bird, and glowing red eyes," she commented.

"Its skin was often reported as charcoal gray or darker, and there were no feathers. It showed up in Point Pleasant in 1966 and scared the daylights out of everybody."

Originally, the press wanted to call the creature Batman, according to Robin, because they thought the wings were shaped more like a bat's. But the Batman television series had recently come out, and that might have created legal complications.

Robin agreed with Susan Sheppard that the Malette/Scarberry encounter at the TNT area wasn't the first, but said that neither was the Partridge event.

"The very first incident is seldom talked about. Very early in November, 1966, some men were digging a grave, and they saw this thing fly over them. They didn't tell anyone because they were afraid everyone would think they were crazy."

That incident took place on November 12, and involved five men at a cemetery in Clendenin, West Virginia, about 80 miles southeast of Point Pleasant. Later, when everyone seemed to be seeing Mothman, and they realized that the coast was clear, the men admitted seeing a creature that looked like "a brown human being," which flew from some nearby trees and glided low over their heads.

What does Mothman really look like?

There are many different drawings, sketches and paintings of Mothman, the most common of which depict a tall, winged figure with no head, just glaring red eyes at shoulder level. Paul asked Robin Bellamy how accurate this portrayal is.

"It actually wasn't like that at all. The muscular body is much more human, with legs and calf muscles," Robin replied. "The Mothman statue in Point Pleasant is a little more realistic, though that has butterfly-like wings."

Robin made the point that many witnesses saw Mothman in the dark, sometimes apparently crouching or sitting, making it look like the creature had no head or neck. In contrast, every witness has mentioned the eyes.

"Consistently, every report talks about the big red eyes. And they don't seem to be reflective. They generate light from within," she said.

Descriptions of Mothman's skin vary considerably, however.

"There's a big discrepancy in the kind of skin or covering people report. Some say it's a leathery skin, others a very fine fur. I suppose it's possible that there are genetic mutations that make one mothman hairier than another."

British UFO researcher Nigel Kerner believes that the "grays," aliens often reported during close encounters, are mechanical or biomechanical. Could the same be true of Mothman? Robin is open to the idea.

"Considering the self-luminescent eyes, and the reports of vertical takeoffs, a mechanical Mothman is possible. But it would have to be a very advanced machine to allow for such ease of movement and no sound."

If Mothman is biomechanical, a combination of machine and living creature, the whole scenario raises even more questions and becomes even more bizarre.

Is Mothman really a precursor of disaster?

"I don't believe that," said Robin in response to a question from Ben. "He's been seen before and after major disasters. But he's also been seen standing in cornfields. But incidents where he's associated with disasters get more press. It's not that exciting to report seeing something strange in a cornfield."

Several people reported seeing Mothman before the I-35 bridge in Minneapolis collapsed on August 1, 2007.

"The media talked about that," Robin said. "And when Mothman was seen on or about 9-11, of course they talked about it. People saw Mothman before the Chernobyl nuclear reactor melted down. But I think that Mothman sightings where negative things are happening are coincidental."

Nevertheless, when the Silver Bridge collapsed on December 15, 1967, "the Mothman reports were just pouring in," Robin said.

"People were seeing him everywhere. We're not talking about teenagers or the town drunk. Witnesses included police officers, lawyers, doctors and other reputable people," she added.

"There are police reports, and somewhere there are casts of footprints. We haven't found them yet, but they're referred to in some of the paperwork the police have."

The Silver Bridge collapse took media attention off Mothman for a time, Robin indicated.

"The bridge collapse devastated the area. Forty-six people died, and some bodies were never recovered. It was a horrendous disaster for a small town. People say that Mothman went away after the bridge fell, but I don't believe that."

Of course, there are plenty of Mothman reports when there are no disasters, she emphasized.

"Mothman is sometimes reported in fields a few weeks before crop circles appear. That happens where I live in Ontario, Canada. We do get these reports from farm communities."

Is Mothman just the icing on the cake?

As for collateral phenomena reported all over the Ohio Valley in the mid-1960s, Robin said these were happening long before Mothman appeared.

"I've absolutely heard those reports. That area has a fair bit of poltergeist activity, UFOs and other odd things anyway. It always has. The first ghost stories date back to the time of (Shawnee) Chief Cornstalk (1720-1777)."

"From Pittsburgh to Louisville along the Ohio River, west to just past Athens, Ohio, there were lots of black triangle UFOs reported, beginning in the mid-1950s."

Interestingly, this area corresponds precisely with the Rome Trough, the geological feature with odd gravitational characteristics that we discuss in our introduction.

How accurate were reports about the MIBs?

"Well, the first one to actually talk about MIBs was the controversial Gray Barker (1925-1984), who wrote about flying saucers. He wrote about MIBs five years before Keel's book," Robin explained.

"There were certainly strange people in Point Pleasant at the time. Remember, this was in the midst of the Cold War, and the Vietnam War was under way."

Robin suggested that suspicions about a possible terrorist or Soviet link to the Mothman happenings, and certainly to the Silver Bridge collapse, might have brought many government people to Point Pleasant.

"As it was, the Army Corps of Engineers had to come and clean up the river after the bridge went down. There were investigators from the National Transportation Safety Board (NTSB), which had just been established that year. And there were a lot of police."

At the same time, Robin acknowledged that there were plenty of oddly-behaved people around.

"I do believe there were some unexplained, people-like things milling around. Their behaviors didn't fit with people we know were there," Robin said. "They'd show up at someone's door in the middle of the night. They'd come in, sit down and ask very strange questions."

Still Kicking

Today, Robin Bellamy gets Mothman reports about every four months, from all over the world. The website Mothmanlives.com has the database.

"There just aren't enough researchers who take this phenomenon seriously," Robin said.

Helped by Mothman?

Nearly all Mothman reports stress how terrified the eyewitnesses were, and sometimes how their lives took turns for the worse after their experiences. Not so with a few witnesses, such as Seattle author and photographer Andrew Colvin, who grew up in the Point Pleasant area.

"My entire family had a Mothman encounter on a back road near Point Pleasant, just before Christmas 1966," Andrew told us when he appeared on *Behind the Paranormal,* adding that he has had ongoing Mothman experiences, many of them psychic and prophetic.

"After my family's experience, suddenly I could draw, sing and take pictures, and I had a photographic memory," Andrew told us.

In fact, he became something of a prodigy, winning a scholarship to Harvard University.

"What is Mothman? That's the toughest question of all," he continued. "Perhaps a denizen of another world, an archetypal deity who shows up in different cultures under different names."

Nevertheless, the symbolism is the same, according to Andrew.

"There's always the hybrid bird/man, with sky symbolism – thunder, lightning, the ether. In the Buddhist world, he represents the background of reality that's sort of alive, the consciousness that undergirds reality through which all the various forms appear that we see. Mothman is a very deep archetype."

Hindus consider him a messenger of God and a guardian of secret knowledge, Andrew pointed out.

"He's caught in the crossfire of religions that want to call him a demon."

Despite the questions and interpretations, and the fact that his initial experience was scary, Andrew is grateful to Mothman.

"I couldn't draw well. After these experiences, I woke up and I could draw like Picasso!"

More Blessings from Mothman

Andrew Colvin wasn't the only Mothman witness to have good things happen. Robin Bellamy has collected many reports.

"I've heard of positive experiences, especially with the math-skills connection. It also depends on the witness's personality," Robin said. "If you see something you would be frightened of anyway, of course the experience is going to be negative. If you're open to new experiences, it could be positive," she declared.

"Some people freak out when they have a ghost sighting. Other people are thrilled."

As we go to press....

In April 2017, people in the Chicago area began reporting a Mothman-like creature. In fact, three separate people reported the flying mystery on the same evening in mid-April, and more witnesses have come forward since then.

Reports have been well recorded by tireless paranormal researcher and our good friend Lon Strickler (Phantomsandmonsters.com). Lon even has an interactive map of the sightings on his excellent website.

Over the weekend of May 20 and 21, a group of people reported hearing an eerie, high-pitched screech. Looking up, they saw not one but two enormous, bat-like creatures circling over a nearby marina.

Two weeks earlier, one of these creatures was reported by an off-duty police officer, out walking with his little boy. The man described a "a distinct human figure about six feet in height" with wings that appeared to be eight to 10 feet across. As of this writing, there have been seven sightings.

Perhaps the name Mothmanlives.com, the website of Jeff Wamsley and the Mothman Museum, is more apt than people realize.

Behind Our Folklore

Every culture on Earth, reaching back to those of our remote ancestors, has legends of gods, demons, angels or just mythical creatures, many of which amount to winged humanoids, whether mothmen or some of the creatures we discuss in Chapter 5.

This aboriginal cave painting in Australia depicts a Mothman-like creature. The painting itself could be as old as 34,000 years. Ivonne Wierink/Shutterstock

Myth and folklore are the vessels of the memory of the human race. Any student of folklore will tell you that every legend that's written on the human psyche -- the inner storybook of our race memory -- is based on something that really happened. No matter how much baggage the story has picked up through the ages, every legend has some grain of truth at its heart. If our distant ancestors encountered what we call Mothman or other flying humanoids, they would have placed supernatiral labels on these creatures that humans could understand. They were angels or demons, depending on the experiences we had with them.

Are we any different today? Modern mythology, including our urban legends, are based on our own limited, materialistic science, which most modern people approach as our ancestors approached religion. Most of us are true believers. So flying humanoids must be so many undiscovered species, hiding just beyond our sight, or mutated animals, bizarre hybrids or even human-made monstrosities, the result of experiments gone wrong.

We suggest that they might be none of the above.

As heard on

CBS Radio – February 6, 2011
WOON 1240 AM – January 5, 2015

The idea that every legend, no matter how outlandish, started with a grain of truth somewhere in the human experience, really isn't that hard to believe. But werewolves?

"'Unknown upright canine cryptids' is a much better term than werewolf," suggested cryptid researcher and prolific author Linda Godfrey when she appeared on *Behind the Paranormal with Paul & Ben Eno.*

In the case of these unknown, upright canines, which are Linda's specialty, "90 percent of the reports don't portray anything that couldn't be a slightly adapted subspecies of a wolf or wolf-dog hybrid."

"Their eyes glow in the headlights, but with the natural yellow or yellow-green eye-shine of a normal canine. They're walking or running on their hind legs, but that's not a supernatural or impossible thing to do. It usually doesn't happen because they aren't built for that. They have to be motivated or trained," Linda told us.

"Otherwise, they're not part human in the sense of sprouting fur and changing into a werewolf. They're walking on toepads like normal dogs, not flat-footed like people or Bigfoot or even bears."

Witnesses report that these canine cryptids have pointed ears on top of their heads, long muzzles, and fangs, according to Linda.

Next page: An artist's conception of Cerberus or Kerberos, also known as the Hound of Hades. In Greek mythology, this terrifying, multi-headed canine guards the gates of the underworld to prevent the dead from leaving. One of the "Twelve Labors of Hercules" was capturing this creature.

Original artwork by Karin Mansberg

"They don't have real shoulders, though sometimes their upper forelimbs are more developed, perhaps because they're hauling around deer carcasses with their newly-freed forelimbs."

These creatures, whatever they are, do strike people as uncanny.

"People feel they're more intelligent than normal animals, and they're just as interested in checking out people as people are in finding out what they are," stated Linda, who averages one to three canine cryptid reports a week.

"Some weeks, I get lots more than that. I tend to get more upright canine reports than I do any other kind. But I do get an amazing amount of Bigfoot reports. I also hear from people who say they've seen huge birds, Mothman types, and water creatures."

A California Wolfman

On the very day of this broadcast, January 5, 2015, Linda received a report of a "wolfman" witnessed by several people in Fresno, California.

"The people were outdoors, and three of them saw this creature, which ran out from behind some trees. It was in full view of the witnesses," Linda reported.

The experiencers stated that the creature was a little larger than an average human, had a very wolf-like head and paws, and was covered with fur. But, below the waist, it was almost furless, with legs that reminded them somewhat of human legs.

"That could be a case of mange, but that doesn't usually occur over only half the body," Linda explained. "A rather chilling aspect of this report was that one witness went dead in the eyes, like he'd gone somewhere else. It took him a minute to come back."

The Dogman
Original Artwork copyright Linda Godfrey, used by permission

The Michigan Dogman

It started as an April Fool's joke and turned into a major cryptozoological incident.

"The term 'Michigan Dogman' was coined in 1987 when a Travers City disk jockey decided to write a song about the Legend of the Dogman. He did it for April Fool's Day," Linda said. "He was going to play the song on the air and sell CDs to benefit a local animal shelter."

The DJ was Steve Cook of WTCM Radio, who described the song as "an amalgam of all the stories I'd heard as a kid."

After he played the song, Steve was amazed when people began calling in and saying they'd actually seen this Dogman, that their grandparents had reported seeing it, and that it was real.

A number of reports of the Dogman have come from the Manstee National Forest area in western Michigan, on the eastern shore of Lake Michigan. And, strangely, from around the Kalamazoo area.

"The Dogman is very like the Beast of Bray Road in Wisconsin," Linda said. "It's a dog-like creature with a long, pronounced muzzle. There are pointy ears on top of the head. It's not a Bigfoot head at all, and it looms like a wolf or dog that can stand and run on two legs," Linda added.

"They're definitely dog-like legs, not like a human, ape or even a bear."

The Dogman also is very aggressive, according to Linda.

"It scares people but seldom hurts them, and the animals people report are identical in almost every case."

Sightings across the United States and Canada date back to the 1930s.

The Beast of Bray Road

Along with being the subject of a rather gory 2005 movie, the Beast of Bray Road, as Linda dubbed it, is practically a neighbor of hers in Elkhorn, Wisconsin. The Beast was first seen in the 1980s on a road that connects two highways just east of that town. It may have existed earlier, however, as a similar upright, canine-like creature was later documented as appearing in 1936 outside Jefferson, Wisconsin (Page 75).

The press has used the same name for many other cryptids seen from the upper Midwest to the Pacific Northwest and Canada.

In December 1991, Linda was a reporter at *The Week* newspaper in Delavan, Wisconsin. That paper is no longer in operation.

"People were seeing what they called a werewolf around a country road in Elkhorn, in southeastern Wisconsin. That's a pretty populated part of state," Linda remembered. "I thought it was crazy, but people were taking it seriously. I poked around and found that our Walworth County animal control officer actually had a file folder that he had labeled 'Werewolf'!"

It turned out that people had been calling this officer to file reports like: "I saw this thing. I don't know what it was! It stood five to seven feet tall, had dark hair all over its body, and ran on hind legs!"

"If there was such a thing as a werewolf, this is what it would look like," Linda quipped.

"The animal control officer didn't know what people were seeing, but he dutifully filed the reports."

The Beast of Bray Road as depicted in a sketch by Linda Godfrey, based on eyewitness descriptions of the Wisconsin canine cryptid. This illustration accompanied the article in which Linda, then a reporter at* The Week *newspaper in Delavan, Wisconsin, broke the story of the Beast in 1991. *Original Artwork copyright Linda Godfrey, used by permission.*

The Monster Hunters

Linda Godfrey

Linda Godfrey

Linda Godfrey is one of the most respected authorities on anomalous animals and paranormal phenomena in America, especially when it comes to sightings in Wisconsin and Michigan.

As a newspaper journalist in the 1990s, Linda was the first to break the story of the terrifying canine cryptid known as the Beast of Bray Road.

She has recorded many other odd happenings in Wisconsin, across the United States and Canada, and even in Britain and Europe.

Linda has written 17 published books on strange creatures, people and phenomena. She has made numerous radio appearances on *Behind the Paranormal with Paul & Ben Eno* and many other media, including *MonsterQuest, Hannity's America, Mysteries and Monsters* and more.

Her website: Lindagodfrey.com.

Linda talked with her editor, who told her that once she had a county official with a file folder, that was news.

"We ran with the story. I was skeptical, but as I talked with people, my skepticism wore down. These were people of all ages and all walks of life," Linda told us.

She realized that there can be some very strange, but perfectly natural, hybrids out there, including wolfdogs and coydogs. But the experiencers seemed to report far more than just an animal.

"Sometimes they felt that there was some kind of awareness, more than an animal, looking back at them," Linda said. "The word I heard most often was 'sneering….' It was sneering at them."

Time and again, witnesses would say they felt the creature knew more than they did, and wanted them to leave.

"People felt almost like they were receiving telepathic messages, like 'don't tell anybody or I'll get you,' or 'You're there and I'm here,' that kind of thing," Linda stated.

As far as she knew, none of the threats was ever followed up on.

"Whatever these animals are, they're very aggressive, and intelligent enough to evade capture," Linda said.

Another Multiversal Creature?

Linda admits that cryptids in general, and the Dogman in particular, could be multiversal or interdimensional creatures. By the way, mutiversal and interdimensional don't mean the same thing. The former means interacting parallel worlds, the latter means various dimensions within one of those worlds.

"We know that we can't see all light waves, and that we can't hear all ranges of sound. Our perceptions are limited," Linda noted. "So what makes us think there aren't creatures living in a place we simply can't see most of the time?"

'Gadara'

One night in 1936, a night security guard, Mark Schackelman, was making his outdoor rounds when he came upon a huge, upright canine cryptid that was apparently digging a hole in an old Indian burial mound. The creature turned around and looked at the guard. The man was petrified, and he started to pray.

According to the guard, the creature seemed fearful for a moment, then croaked something that sounded like "Gadara," in a low, guttural voice.

Schackelman described the creature as huge, human-like, black, and said it had a putrid smell. He also described long, claw-like fingers, along with sharp, canine teeth, pointed ears and a muzzle-like nose.

"The creature slowly disappeared into the nearby woods," Linda said.

The only context we can think of for the word "Gadara" is from the Gospel of Matthew in the New Testament, where Jesus is reported to have cast a number of demons out of a man in the country of the Gadarenes, or Gadara. The demons went into a herd of swine, which ran down the hill and drowned themselves in the Sea of Galilee. Problem is, Gadara is 30 miles from the water. The same incident is reported in the Gospels of Mark and Luke, but in different geographical places.

One possibility is that Schackelman was a religious man, assumed that the creature was a demon, and just thought he heard it say "Gadara." In any case, the same guard reported seeing the same creature the following night.

Linda Godfrey pointed out that this took place within the mere 13-square-mile area she refers to as the Jefferson County Square of Weirdness.

"Along with the Beast of Bray Road and other canine cryptids, there are Bigfoot and giant birds, and UFOs galore. There's even a haunted road and a lake monster," Linda told us.

Interestingly, this was a center of the ancient Mississippian culture, a Native American civilization, also known as the Mound Builders, that flourished from about 800 to 1600 CE. There are burial mounds and small pyramids, some of the latter located at the bottom of Rock Lake, home of Rocky the Lake Monster! Tourists can visit ancient mounds in the state park and National Historic Landmark in a town with the exotic name of Aztalan.

"You name it, and it seems to be in the Square of Weirdness," Linda said.

Acknowledging that this is certainly a paranormal flap area, or window area, as John Keel would have called it, Linda pointed out the beliefs of many ancient peoples, including the Native Americans, that creatures like Bigfoot and canine cryptids, which they sometimes referred to as manwolves, are "spirit animals."

"Spirit animals know how to travel back and forth between spirit worlds, or what we would call dimensions or parallel worlds. That's why we never find them," Linda said. "There's a belief that some kind of ancient (power) keeps them from attacking us."

Linda also discussed the Dog Soldiers or Dog Men among the Native Americans, especially the Cheyenne as they resisted the expansion of United States influence into Kansas, Nebraska, Colorado and Wyoming in the early 19th century.

The Dog Soldiers were essentially a military society, with highly effective combat units that perfected guerilla warfare on the American plains. They also reflected a tendency of the Native Americans, as their control over their native lands faded, to become more mystical.

"The Dog Soldiers represented a special totem as protectors of the people," Linda stated. "If they died in battle, they could come back as spirit creatures to guard sacred places."

Such as the ancient mounds in the Square of Weirdness, we wonder?

About Those Hind Legs

How could canines, spirit creatures, guardians or not, walk, let alone run, on their hind legs for any length of time when not physically built to do so? Unless, of course, they really are half human.

"I'm not prepared to say that," Linda responded. "I don't believe in the classic werewolf. I don't believe that humans can physically change, to grow fur and have their teeth lengthen, their muzzles contort, and their spines elongate. That's way too impossible."

At the same time, Linda is convinced that hind-leg locomotion is no insurmountable problem.

"You'd be surprised how well mammals can get around on their hind legs when they're motivated. Bears are a good example. They'll stand on their hind legs and look at you, and take a few steps. For centuries, they've been trained to do 'dancing bear' acts."

While she is neither a canine nor a cryptid, Ben Eno's cat, Clementine, demonstrates that quadrupeds can easily walk on their hind legs when motivated.

Linda cited a YouTube™ video of a bear with cubs and an injured forelimb.

"The bear had to walk upright out of necessity. Then there's the famous Merengue Dancing Dog, trained to beautifully dance on her hind legs. Faith the Wonder Dog was born without front legs, and has been trained to walk on hind legs alongside her owner."

· But why would mammals, especially wolves, walk on their hind legs in the wild, where there certainly are no people training them to do it?

"Walking upright provides a few advantages," Linda said. "For example, if you can carry prey away with your forelimbs, you're less likely to have another predator grab it while you're dragging it. Or, in an environment with tall grasses, you would be able to see something coming at you. You can see more. Of course, this is mere speculation on my part. Native Americans simply say they are shape-shifters."

Not Very Human

"Witnesses describe these creatures as almost entirely canine," said Linda. "But they'll say it did have claws on its paws, not hands, but paws that seemed slightly elongated. That would seem to be a good adaptation if you stood upright and wanted to carry things. You can understand the work of natural selection in an adaptation like that."

"If we have a mutation like this in the wild population, why isn't it reported more frequenly, and why aren't these canines dancing down country roads?" Paul asked.

"They can just as easily go on all fours," Linda replied. In fact. witnesses say that when these cryptids realize they're being observed, they drop to all fours. But there are also reports of canines that are on all fours, then stand up and run away on two legs."

Linda emphasized that, "These canine cryptids are elusive, don't like to have their pictures taken, but other than that, I have no explanation. When there are photos, they're almost always blurry."

A typical conception of a man turning into a werewolf. Strangely enough, the final result matches one of the most common descriptions of a canine cryptid. Camilkuo/Shutterstock

Linda Godfrey's Own Sighting

In her long years of research, has Linda herself ever seen a canine cryptid?

"Yes, I believe I saw part of a dogman," she replied.

"I was in the field, filming *MonsterQuest: Hunting the American Werewolf* with the History Channel. We were on a lonely, desolate road at 3 a.m., with witnesses who had seen a seven-foot, grayish, doglike creature that ran upright, and a smaller, dark-brown one."

The camera crew had a spotlight trained on an area where green eye-shine had been seen in the bushes.

"We heard something running around in there, then something like a huge dog shaking its fur," Linda reported. "I happened to turn just as something hit the edge of the spotlight. You could just see the fur on its back illuminated for just a moment. It was gray and it was vertical."

Linda swears that the creature was running upright.

"It momentarily blocked out a road sign. When we measured the sign, the creature would have had to be seven feet tall."

Unfortunately, the camera was turned in another direction, as usually happens.

"Maybe it knew that, and chose that moment to run," Linda speculated. "The witnesses got crazy scared and wanted to leave immediately."

4 SEA AND LAKE MONSTERS

As heard on

Achieve Radio January 18, 2009
WOON 1240 AM August 16, 2009, October 4, 2009
CBS Radio -October 22, 2010, July 14, 2013

It's often been said that we know more about the surface of the moon than we do about our own oceans. That's true, but we're constantly learning more, some of it rather disconcerting.

In the late 1970s, ocean scientists excitedly announced the discovery of volcanic geothermal vents on the ocean floor off South America. In ensuing years, scientists have found more and more of these sites, at which seawater that has seeped down to the molten rock far below is superheated and forced back through the vents into the sea.

Marine biologists, who had always assumed that the sun ultimately powered all biology on Earth, were flummoxed to discover hundreds of new species around these vents. They were entirely unknown life forms, dependent not on the sun, as we are, but on (to us) deadly hydrogen sulfide. And, in the vicinity of the volcanic vents, these creatures were living in searing temperatures, sometimes as high as 700 degrees (F).

This led to a complete rethink of where life can be found and what unexpected forms it might take.

During a 2014 expedition to the Mariana Trench, an international research team, led by two University of Hawaii scientists, found a thriving community of animals, including a new species of the deepest fish ever recorded. Bear in mind that the Mariana Trench, located in the western Pacific near the Mariana Islands, is the deepest point of the world's oceans. At its maximum depth, the crescent-shaped trench is well over 36,000 feet deep, and water pressure is almost 16,000 pounds per square inch.

A typical sea serpent as described not only by sailors but also by high-ranking naval officers in the 18th and 19th centuries. Original artwork by Karin Mansberg

Blackie makes an appearance

At least we understand rivers and lakes, right? Strangely enough, lakes and rivers can be just as mysterious.

It was a pleasant October 2, 2016, when co-author Paul Eno was strolling

Paul Eno captured these photos of a creature in the Blackstone River in Lincoln, Rhode Island, in October, 2016, from about 20 feet away. In photo 1, thrashing in the water attracts Paul's attention. In photo 2, a head the size of a football rises out of the water and gives Paul a dirty look. In photo 3, the creature turns away and, in photo 4, it submerges. Paul and friends at the Rhode Island Dept. of Environmental Management, to whom he showed the photos, are not certain what this was. But speculation has included a snapping turtle of record-breaking size, a freed pet python that has grown in the wild or -- Blackie?

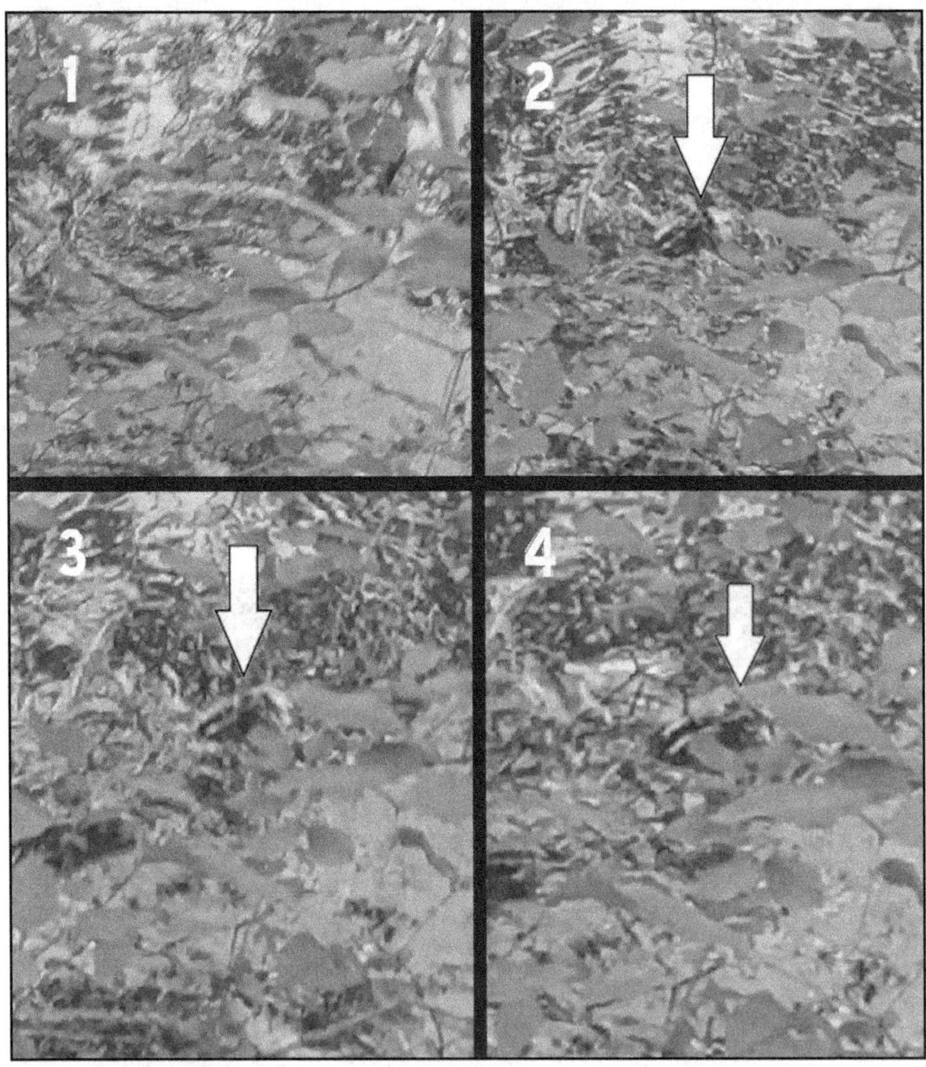

along the Blackstone Valley Bikeway in Lincoln, Rhode Island.

"Suddenly, in the river, to my left and about 20 feet away, there was a thrashing by some large creature in the water," Paul said. "I always keep my smart-phone camera app active as I walk there, because there's always something interesting to see."

There usually isn't something as interesting as Paul saw that day, however. As he described it, a head the size of a football rose out of the water at the end of a long neck, stared at him, turned, then submerged.

"I know it saw me," Paul recalled. "And I felt – the best word is 'unwelcome.'"

Paul sent the photos to two friends at the Rhode Island Department of Environmental Management, one of whom was a biologist. After joking about the debut of "Blackie" the river monster, the opinion was mixed.

"This could very well have been a huge snapping turtle," Paul said. "There are some in the Blackstone River, but the head wasn't right. And I've lived by rivers all my life. This would be the biggest snapping turtle I've ever heard of, by far."

There was also some speculation that this could have been a huge python.

"There have been stories in the media about people releasing pet pythons into the wild, especially in the South, where they can grow to enormous sizes. This could have been the case with 'Blackie,' but that would be unusual in New England, where they would never survive the winters."

Paul said that, whatever this was, it stirred up the water for 10 feet in every direction, and there was no sign of any turtle shell.

A Chinese River Monster?

On May 27, 2017, just before this book went to press, a strange video arrived from China. It seemed to show a huge creature breaking the surface of the Zhelin Reservoir, near the city of Jiujiang, taken from the Mount Lu Xihai Resort.

As of this writing, the video was available on YouTube™ at https://www.youtube.com/watch?v=Ob8FC0mw3Cs.

The Great New England Sea Serpent

"There are many kinds of lake and sea monsters, from 'Nessie' in Scotland to 'Ogopogo' in Canada," said prolific author and researcher Jeremy Robinson (Page 85) when he appeared on *Behind the Paranormal with Paul & Ben Eno.* The subject of the show was the Great New England Sea Serpent, reported now and then for centuries off the coasts of Massachusetts and Maine. At least once, it has been seen on shore.

Witnessed, sometimes by crowds of people, from 1638 to the last reported sighting in 1997, the creature or creatures was/were huge.

"We have some very good descriptions. It was dark on top, and white beneath, and between 50 and 200 feet long. People in earlier centuries often compared the thickness of creatures like serpents to barrels and kegs," Jeremy explained. "People also described a horse-shaped head."

One witness described the creature as "like a string of gallon kegs 100 feet long."

The first sighting was on -- as opposed to off -- Cape Ann, Massachusetts, in 1638, with a second sighting in 1641, according to Jeremy.

"The first sighting was by four people, two Native Americans and two Englishmen," he said.

Oddly enough, the creature was out of the water, coiled on a rock, while the humans were out on the water, passing by in a boat.

"The Indians, who seemed to know all about the creature, warned against shooting it, because that would put all their lives in danger," said Jeremy. "The Englishmen didn't shoot it."

A woman standing on the far shore thought the creature was a fallen tree. After the men passed, the creature slid back into the water.

There have been more than 200 reports, according to Jeremy, a *New York Times* bestselling author, whose novel *Kronos* is a fictionalized thriller about the Great New England Sea Serpent, set in present time.

"The creature was seen by up to 200 people at a time, from ships. The most recent sighting was reported in 1997, but it was most widely seen in 1917, when there were 18 reported sightings, mostly in and around Gloucester Harbor," said Jeremy.

Up to that time, there were 22 reported sightings, he indicated.

On the air, Paul read an affidavit, sworn to in August 1817, by one Matthew Gaffney, a ship's carpenter.

> **That on the 14th day of August, A.D. 1817, between the hours of four and five o'clock in the afternoon, I saw a strange marine animal, resembling a serpent in the harbor in said Gloucester. I was in a boat and was within 30 feet of him. His head appeared full as large as a four-gallon keg, his body as large as a barrel, and his length that I saw I should judge 40 feet at least. The top of his head was of a dark color and the underpart of his head appeared nearly white, as did also several feet of his belly that I saw... I fired at him when he was the nearest to me....**

Gaffney then reported that the creature, apparently unaffected by the shot, turned on him, as if to attack the boat. Instead, it sank like a rock, resurfacing

The Monster Hunters

Jeremy Robinson

Jeremy Robinson

Even though he's primarily a novelist, Jeremy Robinson is an authority on the Great New England Sea Serpent, a creature witnessed by more people than many cryptids that are far better known.

Jeremy was born in the sometimes mysterious seacoast town of Beverly, Massachusetts, which is on the coast north of Boston, not far from Salem. His father encouraged a love for science fiction.

A resident of New Hampshire, Jeremy is the international bestselling author of more than 50 novels and novellas, including the Jack Sigler thriller series. He is also known as the #1 Amazon.com horror writer Jeremy Bishop, author of *The Sentinel*, and Jeremiah Knight, author of the post-apocalyptic *Hunger* series.

His novels have been translated into 13 languages. In the pastoral calm of the Granite State, Jeremy continues to write novels.

His website: Bewareofmonsters.com.

about 100 yards away. According to Gaffney, the creature moved quickly, at a rate of a mile every two to three minutes.

"I'd say that sturdy fisherfolk like Gaffney would have much more credibility than tourists," Jeremy said..

A Surfeit of Serpents

"How could such a large creature move so quickly in the water?" Paul asked Jeremy.

"Most people said it had fins, but moved vertically up and down like a snake," Jeremy replied.

As for the credibility of the sightings, "People were less skeptical, in general, in those days," Jeremy continued. "But many of the sightings were by sailors who spent most of their lives on the sea. Today, people are more skeptical because we've had a lot of hoaxes."

Unlike today, there was no money to be made in monsters, he pointed out.

"In those days, people risked reputations and ridicule, but sailors don't mistake dolphins for sea serpents."

Once again, Jeremy emphasized just how little was known about the sea, then and now.

"Just in 2007, we got our first glimpse of a giant squid. And that's a 40-foot creature. It's very possible that this creature (the sea serpent) could be in the ocean, and has not been seen long enough for us to record it. The existence of the giant squid was doubted by scientists for decades."

In fact, the first video of a giant squid in its underwater environment wasn't captured until 2013.

"The giant squid is big, but reports of the Great New England Sea Serpent averaged 100 feet, and there were reports that it was up to 200 feet. That would make it the largest creature in the ocean," Jeremy said.

"Why no sightings since 1997?" Paul asked.

"The assumption has to be that there was a population to sustain the species," Jeremy answered. "Probably they were feeding on something that was plentiful at the time, but now it's not there. The whole area of the Gulf of Maine has been very overfished, and there isn't much fishing going on there now. So the creatures either moved to a better feeding ground or died out."

He cited the advantages of research done as places like Loch Ness, as opposed to the Gulf of Maine.

"A lot of research has been done at Loch Ness. It's a big lake. But the ocean is much bigger. Creatures would be harder to find, despite their size, and it would depend on random sightings. With lakes, we can use fish-finding devices."

This makes it even harder to convince scientists that the sea serpent actually exists.

"I don't think that even a photo can convince the scientific community."

Meg

Dr. Steve Alten (Page 87), author of the popular *MEG* series of novels, featuring that lovable, 70-foot, 70,000-pound cousin of the great white shark, the megalodon, appeared on the show to talk about possible survivals of this creature, thought to be extinct for at least 10,000 years.

Ben Eno pointed out that "new species are found every day, and species thought to be extinct are found often."

"That's right," Steve agreed. "Seventy percent of our planet is covered by ocean, and only three to five percent has been explored. We don't know what's down there, especially in the deeper waters. We certainly have fossilized meg teeth by the thousands."

As for megalodon, "this is the shark that ate the shark in *Jaws*," Steve quipped.

Paul and Ben both wanted to know if there had been any sightings.

"There have been sightings of large dorsal fins over the last 100 years," Steve

The Monster Hunters

Steve Alten

Steve Alten

One of the few fiction writers ever to appear on *Behind the Paranormal with Paul & Ben Eno*, Dr. Steve Alten is the *New York Times* bestselling author of the *MEG* series and many other novels.

In doing research for the books, Steve became an expert on the prehistoric monster shark, *carcharodon megalodon*, believed to have been extinct for over 10,000 years.

MEG would go on to become the book of the 1996 Frankfurt Book Fair, where it eventually sold to readers in more than 20 countries. *MEG* hit every major bestseller list, including #19 on the *New York Times* list (#7 audio), and became a popular radio series in Japan.

Several of Steve's books have been, or are being made, into feature films. His website: Stevealten.com.

replied. "One report claimed that a giant shark destroyed crayfish pots in Alaska. There was another sighting off Australia, but nothing that can be corroborated."

He speculated that a huge shark like the megalodon could inhabit the "midwaters," 3,000 to 5,000 feet down, "and there's no reason to surface and show us the telltale dorsal fin."

Paul mentioned the 35,000-foot dive into the Mariana Trench by the bathyscaphe *Trieste* in 1960, a feat that wasn't repeated, as far as we know, for decades.

"They supposedly saw giant sharks, but that wasn't reported," Steve said.

Like Jeremy Robinson, Steve also cited the biological surprises the sea has served up since the 1970s.

"Prior to 1977, scientists would say there was no life at the bottom of the ocean because there's no light. The (deep-diving submarine) *Alvin* dove, only to find chemosythesis-based life in 700-degree (F) water around these geothermal vents at the bottom, and an entirely new ecosystem."

Steve noted that, after his novel *MEG*, the first in that series, was released in 1997, scientists lowered video cameras in 6,000 feet of water, and discovered a new species of shark, 28 feet long.

Above, if the megalodon shark, which makes its direct descendant, the great white shark, look like a guppy, and is thought to have been extinct for at least the last 10,000 years, isn't extinct after all, this is what it would look like if it surfaced next to a man and a boat. Below is a 45 million-year-old megalodon tooth.

"Megalodon hunted whales, and near coastal areas, when they were thriving. Their teeth have been found in ocean-access riverbeds and lagoons on the Carolina and Georgia coasts."

Megalodon would have one natural enemy, Steve said.

"That would be a pod of a dozen or more orcas. The only escape for megalodon would have been to go deep. So if that's where the megs went, we'd never know they were there. There may still be some out there, and that's scary."

The Sea vs. the Lake

Steve noted the most common differences between sea and lake cryptids, as reported by witnesses.

"Creatures reported at sea are most often sea serpents, whereas lake monsters tend to be more like the plesiosaur," Steve said. "Still the horse-like head is common in reports of both."

Nessie and Champ

The undisputed monarch of all lake monsters is certainly the creature or creatures reported in Scotland's deep, dark, 23-mile-long Loch Ness. Sightings of "Nessie" have been reported there as far back as the 6th century, and they still occur several times a year.

Trouble is, the conditions at Loch Ness are tailor-made to trick the eye, from

The most common description of the Loch Ness Monster, and many other lake cryptids, matches that of a prehistoric water predator known as the plesiosaur. Victor Habbick/Shutterstock

The Monster Hunters

Nick Redfern

Nick Redfern

Nick Redfern is the author of 43 books on UFOs, cryptozoology, zombies and Hollywood scandal, including *The Roswell UFO Conspiracy*, *Women in Black, Men in Black*, and *365 Days of UFOs.* Nick has appeared on many TV shows, including the BBC's *Out of This World*, the SyFy Channel's *Proof Positive*, the History Channel's *MonsterQuest*, *America's Book of Secrets*, *Ancient Aliens* and *UFO Hunters*, the National Geographic Channel's *Paranatural*, and MSNBC's *Countdown with Keith Olbermann*, and he has been a guest many times on *Behind the Paranormal with Paul & Ben Eno.*

Among his many adventures, Nick has investigated reports of lake monsters in Scotland, vampires in Puerto Rico, werewolves in England, aliens in Mexico, and sea serpents in the United States. He travels and lectures around the world. Originally from Staffordshire, England, he currently lives in Arlington, Texas.

His website: Nickredfernfortean.blogspot.com

the low-visibility, peat-filled water to the strange lighting effects caused by the interplay of wave, sun and mountainside. Distance and size are difficult to gauge, so an otter swimming across the loch, creating a long wake, or even a gust of wind, can be and have been mistaken for the monster. Another factor is the known presence of a population of enormous eels in the loch.

Still, when it comes to water monsters, Loch Ness is the world's most scrutinized lake, and by some very qualified people.

Dr. Roy Mackal (1925-2013) was a University of Chicago biologist with a keen interest in Nessie, and he was involved in the first sonar sweeps of the loch in the 1970s. Findings were inconclusive, due in large part to the heavy presence of floating plant debris at all levels of the loch, which at one point is as deep as 889 feet. At the same time, Mackal himself was convinced that something strange lived in the loch, especially after his own sighting in 1970.

In his 1976 book *The Monsters of Loch Ness*, Mackal suggested that there is a population of large, previously unknown amphibians, later revising that to prehistoric zeuglodons and/or serpentine whales, both believed to be extinct for millions of years.

Where do they come from and how do they survive?

In one of his many appearances on *Behind the Paranormal with Paul & Ben Eno*, paranormal Renaissance man, energetic author and monster hunter Nick Redfern (Page 90) agreed with Mackal on the population question.

"There has to be a breeding population at Loch Ness," Nick said, noting that photos that show humps in the water probably indicate several creatures feeding at the same time, their heads below the surface. "You see that all the time with orcas and dolphins," he added.

"People talk about the Loch Ness Monster as though it's a single creature. But we have to be talking about a colony of creatures. It has to be a viable size so they can breed."

Nick also noted, as have many researchers, that Loch Ness, though its surface is 52 feet above sea level, is thought to have at least one underground outlet to the sea, though some scientists dispute this. Such an outlet would be a major factor in allowing a population of large creatures to come and go, maintaining breeding capability.

"Until the last ice age, Loch Ness and several other lochs were all open to the ocean," Nick Redfern noted. "When the lochs were landlocked during the last ice age, whatever was in there wouldn't have been able to get out. That's the official story, anyway."

However, a glance at the map shows Loch Ness at the center of a long, glacial scar that runs diagonally from the North Sea to the Atlantic Ocean.

"There are rumors, and some evidence, that, maybe deep under the loch, some of the entrance points from the ocean might not have been completely blocked. So, possibly, these things can still come and go," said Nick.

Even in Little Lakes

The British Isles are dotted with glacial lakes, many of them quite small but extraordinarily deep. Monster reports come from many of these.

Seven members of the Coyne family, peat farmers near Connemara in the County of Galway in western Ireland, watched a lengthy performance by a large creature in Lough Nahooin, from sunset until nightfall, on February 22, 1968.

Farmer Stephen Coyne was the first to notice "something black in the water." As Coyne and his young son watched it, they could see a long neck with a round, horse-like head nearly a foot in diameter, and with horn-like protuberances. They also saw a flat tail and what appeared to be slick, slippery black skin.

According to the Coynes, the creature seemed to swim back and forth aimlessly, until the family dog began barking at it. Then the creature turned and swam toward the Coynes, with its mouth open and in an aggressive poise. When Coyne made the dog stop barking, the creature turned away, and continued swimming aimlessly.

The rest of the Coyne family soon ran down to the lough to see the creature, noting that it was about 12 feet long and had two humps on its back. Most bizarre of all, the creature appeared to have no eyes. They reported that, at one point, the tail flipped up, almost touching the head.

The absence of eyes got our attention. If true, this characteristic could mean that the creature's natural habitat was in lightless caverns far underground. It might have found its way to the surface in this part of Ireland, which is filled with caves and underground rivers.

The British Isles aren't the only places with lake monsters. Many other European countries, including Iceland and Russia, have their own creatures and legends.

Monsters and the Military

"The British government keeps a file on sea and lake monsters. This is publicly accessible at the National Archives at Kew, near London. There are thousands of declassified documents," Nick Redfern said.

The Sea Serpents File runs from about 1830 to 1880.

"It's filled with reports from Royal Navy personnel, and it's packed with reports from the Atlantic Ocean, many from around the area of St. Helena, a volcanic island in the South Atlantic Ocean," Nick explained.

The sheer number of reports suggests that a colony of these cryptids lived or lives in the sea around the island.

"Many of these reports don't talk about vague things seen in the distance, and that could have been whales or sharks," said Nick. "These are things seen from 50 or 100 feet away, from the wooden warships of the day, with the captain and crew leaning over the side of a ship, seeing these gigantic creatures."

In some cases, the reports describe creatures 250-300 feet long, according to Nick.

"That's incredible! They describe bodies like a typical serpent, with a large head and powerful neck standing upright, out of the water. In some cases, they're described as having a mane, not hairy, but like strands of skin flowing down the back. We often hear that in lake monsters, too," he continued.

"When credible military personnel report sightings that close and that large, it's difficult to come to any other conclusion: What they described is what they saw."

Lake Monsters as Military Decoys?

Nick told us a fascinating story of military involvement with lake monsters.

"I've found evidence from both U.S. and U.K. sources that both countries used lake monsters to actually hide military programs," he said. "In one case in the U.S., in the '40s and '50s, experiments were being done in various lakes using small, remote-controlled submersibles. They were highly advanced."

People reported seeing these fast-moving objects breaking the surface of the lakes, according to Nick.

"So the military actually started spreading lake-monster stories. They weren't investigating monsters, but using the stories to carry out a cover-up."

Even seals got into the act.

"In Wales, before World War I, the British military were trying to train seals to carry explosives," said Nick.

This was at Bala Lake (*Llyn Tegid* in the Cymric language of Wales), which today is thought of as the home of Teggie the Terror of the Lake. In fact, the story of the monster probably began with the seals.

"Late at night, the military people were there, and people would see large animals swimming around. The lake-monster story spread, encouraged by the military," Nick stated.

"I'm not suggesting that there aren't genuine lake monsters. There are good and strong, credible stories of them!"

Champ

Beneath the long and beautiful Lake Champlain, which straddles the three-way border between Vermont, New York and Quebec, dwells, supposedly, the creature affectionately known as Champ, whose description matches Nessie's rather closely. The lake shore is well populated, from Vermont's largest city, Burlington, and along both shores, which include many farms and summer cottages.

Champ has a long history. Supposedly, the French explorer Samuel de Champlain (1567-1635), from whom the lake takes its name, saw the monster himself in 1609. The most reliable reports, however, begin about 1819, when residents near Port Henry, New York, reported seeing the creature in Bulwagga Bay.

Things were quiet until 1871, when a group of sightseers were shocked by what they said was an appearance by the creature in Horseshoe Bay, on the Vermont side. Not long afterward, passengers aboard the steamer *Curlew* reported a long neck, topped by a horse-like head, and leaving a wake up to 40 feet long.

None other than the great circus showman P.T. Barnum heard about all this, and, in 1873, he put up a reward of $50,000 for anyone who could catch the "sea serpent," whose hide he intended to display at the New York State Capitol

Lake Champlain, seen from the Vermont farm country south of Burlington, looking across to the Adirondack Mountains of New York State. *Melanie Bishop/Shutterstock*

in Albany.

There were no takers. But Champ continued to appear on his (or her) own terms.

In July 1880, two men, a Dr. Brigham and Mr. Shelters, reportedly saw the creature in Missiquoi Bay, at the Quebec end of the lake. They later stated that "portions of its body 20 feet in length appeared above the surface of the water."

They described the creature's head as "large as a flour barrel," "of irregular shape," and its eyes as "having a greenish tinge."

Another major sighting was reported in 1873 by no less a dignitary than Nathan H. Mooney, sheriff of Clinton County, New York, an officer in the Union Army during the Civil War who had fought at Fredericksburg.

According to the good sheriff, watching from about 50 yards away, the creature "raised its head four or five feet out of the rough water." It was 25 feet long, and the neck was about seven inches across. Mooney specifically mentioned muscles relaxing and contracting in the creature's neck, which was "curved like that of a goose."

A report from 1899 went one better. That's because Champ was seen on land.

A local resident at Cumberland Head, New York, claimed that the creature, matching the usual plesiosaur-like description, was on the shore, about six feet out of the water. Interestingly, Champ was described as dark to black on top and lighter-colored beneath.

By the early 1980s, there were over 130 reports, 33 of which included the long neck.

By 1975, a young social studies teacher from Wilton, New York, Joseph W. Zarzynski, author of *Champ: Beyond the Legend* (1988) and several other books, threw himself into the problem of finding the creature. In ensuing years, he has assembled a mountain of reports and done considerable research, almost entirely at his own expense.

In the late 1970s, Zarzynski joined James Kennard of Rochester Engineering Laboratories in a project that used high-tech sonar gear to search for Champ. On June 3, 1979, they reported readings indicating the presence of a 10- to 15-foot-long, moving object in the lake beneath their boat.

Zarzyski continues to find tantalizing but inconclusive evidence.

"I've spoken with witnesses who have lived in the area all their lives. Some who lived there 20 or 30 years have seen Champ, and they said they'd never seen anything like it," Nick Redfern told us.

As with Loch Ness, Nick pointed out, Champlain and other large lakes can be subject to significant wave disturbances that create formations that look like large humps in the water.

"But lifetime residents know that and should be able to differentiate," said Nick. "Experienced witnesses are important."

Lexie

Another New England lake that supposedly has its own monster is Alexander Lake in Killingly, Connecticut, home of Lexie. In this case, however, we have some inside information in the person of our cousin-in-law, Bill Bessette of nearby Moosup, Connecticut, a native of the area who has had a summer home on Lake Alexander for many years. Bill is an avid fisherman and has spent countless hours angling from a boat on the 215-acre glacial lake.

"Years ago, there was a guy fishing from his dock, across the lake from where we live," Bill told us. "He claims he hooked something huge that almost pulled him into the water. Whatever it was, he never landed it."

Bill, who doesn't believe for a minute that Lexie exists, says that incident started the monster legend. Over the years, wind-whipped water, floating logs and wishful thinking have added to the legend.

"The darn lake is only 25 feet deep!" Bill summed up.

The Flathead Lake Monster

One of America's most classic, but least known, lake monsters reportedly lives in the 188-square mile Flathead Lake in northwestern Montana. Complete

The authors and their relatives frolic on Alexander Lake in Killingly, Connecticut, on the Fourth of July, 2009. Just across the lake occurred the incident that prompted the story of the Alexander Lake Monster. *Photo by Paul Eno*

with a set of rolling humps on the lake surface, the creature is said to be eel-like and 20-30 feet long, with a large, horse-like head.

As many as 102 sightings had been reported between 1899 and 2013. Terrified swimmers have reported being grazed by the creature, and boaters have had encounters with a seemingly curious monster.

More than one creature has been reported at the same time, suggesting a breeding population.

What are they?

"The most popular belief is that these lake monsters are surviving creatures from the dinosaur era, like plesiosaurs," Nick Redfern told us. "Many of the characteristics people talk about, like the hump, the long neck and the flippers, do sound like plesiosaurs. Those predatory creatures did exist."

Nick pointed out that, whatever these animals are, local legends about them often go back to the remote past.

"Some people believe that they're some form of gigantic, mutated eel, up to 40 feet long," he said. "These creatures are often seen on land, and eels can leave the water and move on land. A gigantic eel isn't really a monster, but if you meet something that big, it can certainly seem like one. But, whatever it is, I'm sure it will turn out to be pretty extraordinary if we ever get the solid evidence."

Hoaxes and Blurry Photos

All the headliners among monsters have been the subject of hoaxers, and there are very few clear photos, even from credible witnesses, perhaps because of the strange electromagnetic conditions created at world boundaries, as we've discussed in previous chapters.

"When you get rid of the hoaxes, the misidentifications and the blurry photos, there is a body of evidence that these creatures exist," Nick stated, stressing the importance of on-site, first-hand investigations.

"With cryptozoology, of all paranormal subjects, it's important to be there. If we stake out these locations, we actually stand a good chance of seeing something and gathering some eveidence," he said.

"Ghost and UFO sightings are random. But with lakes, there's a limited area, and that can work in our favor."

5 HUMANOIDS

As heard on

WOON 1240 Radio – September 6, 2010, October 30, 2016, January 15, 2017
CBS Radio – July 29, 2012

Let's enter an area of cryptozoology where many lines blur, and we don't necessarily mean the lines between parallel worlds. As we often say on *Behind the Paranormal with Paul & Ben Eno*, our language isn't really up to actually talking about things like the paranormal. We and our folklore have applied labels from our narrow paradigm to entities and phenomena that are way beyond it.

Certainly we can tell the difference between the Great New England Sea Serpent and Bigfoot. But Bigfoot can also be considered a humanoid, as can many human-like creatures we might consider space aliens, wolfmen, mothmen, or things that we don't even have names for yet.

We might get beyond commonly-accepted cryptids and into territories usually associated with ghost studies or with parasite (demon and poltergeist) research and mitigation, such as "shadow people" or archetypal figures like the "slender man," the "little blonde girl" or the "man in the checkered shirt."

"A humanoid is an entity or creature that in most aspects resembles a human, but has certain differences," said Albert Rosales (Page 100), tireless chronicler of strange events, when he appeared on the show. "They have two arms, two legs and a head. But, according to my catalog here, there are thousands of different types of humanoids reported worldwide. It's not only the little gray humanoids (aliens) we are so familiar with in Hollywood films."

Albert, based in Florida, maintains what we believe is the world's largest database of humanoid encounters, at Ufoinfo.com/humanoid. And it keeps growing: Albert receives 20 to 30 new humanoid reports each day, he told us.

"What's the most common experience that people report?" Paul Eno asked.

"Lately, the most common type I've found is what I call the bedroom visitation," Albert replied. "You wake up in the middle of the night, and you may feel paralyzed. There's something there in the bedroom with you, and it might be short or tall, but that's been very common lately."

Albert also has received many reports of shadow people or creatures.

"Short humanoids with large heads have been popular lately, and have been reported since the 1980s. There are all different types of humanoids reported."

The Multiverse Revisited?

"The parallel world idea makes total sense," Albert said. "With most of these humanoids, there's more of an interdimensional connection than an interstellar one. I think we're dealing more with beings or visitations from multiple worlds."

At the same time, Albert said this doesn't mean that some humanoids couldn't be coming from other planets, perhaps even using parallel worlds to travel here.

"Some can be confused with ghosts or whatever, and that's where it can be hard to keep our bearings."

A Beard and a Helmet

Albert himself had a humanoid encounter when he was a boy growing up in Cuba.

"I was walking down the hallway in my home, and I looked in the mirror. I saw the figure of a man, and I clearly remember he had a beard, a helmet, and he was smiling. Somehow he resembled an old Spanish soldier," said Albert.

"I don't know what type of humanoid this was, but it was definitely there and it scared me. Of course, my mother paid no attention to me."

If convinced that they weren't imagining the whole thing, the first thought for most experiencers would be, "Aha! A ghost!" But, as we've pointed out in other books, the spirit of a dead person is probably the least likely explanation for what we, without thinking, assume are ghosts in the classic sense of the word. The laws of physics in our world simply wouldn't allow it. And why would the man appear to have a body and clothing, let alone a helmet, if he was a spirit – by definition, a disembodied being?

Even though they appear to be from our past, humans or humanoids like this could be people from a parallel world where the laws of physics are different, and allow awareness of, and even communication with, their multiversal neighbors. Or, in a deeper sense of the term than we're used to, he could have been a time traveler. It's even possible that the man was a different version of Albert himself, and that's why he appeared in a mirror.

The Monster Hunters
Albert Rosales

Albert Rosales

Albert S. Rosales has been collecting data on humanoids, entities, extraterrestrials, UFOnauts, and just about every other kind of strange being since the 1980s. His books include *UFOs over Florida: Humanoid and other Strange Encounters in the Sunshine State*, and the 16-book series *Humanoid Encounters: The Others Amongst Us*, which covers humanoid cases from ancient times to 2015.

Born in Cuba, Albert migrated to the United States in 1966. He had several unusual incidents as a young man while still living in Cuba, and more as an adult in America.

Albert became interested in unusual phenomena and UFOs at a young age. His database currently contains over 18,000 cases, and it is updated and corrected daily. Along with *Humanoid Encounters*, he has written four books so far, and more are expected soon.

"I pay tribute to all the great authors and UFOlogists who came before me: Jacques Vallee, J. Allen Hynek, Carol and Jim Lorenzen, Gordon Creighton, Frank Edwards, Jerome Clark, etc.," Albert said. "...They helped guide me in my weird and wonderful quest, a lonely quest at times, perhaps not understood by most, but something I feel compelled to do. I think it is and will be important."

His website: Ufoinfo.com/humanoid. Contact Albert at garuda79@att.net.

In multiversal, multi-faceted reality, other versions of ourselves are always present in our subconscious minds, and they can sometimes become conscious.

"Many times in these experiences, you hardly notice what happened," Albert explained. "It doesn't register right away. Later on, you go, 'wait a minute.'"

The man in the mirror was neither the first nor the last of Albert's experiences.

"In Cuba, in 1963 and 1964, there were a lot of electrical blackouts. One time when this happened, there was a big, bright object, like a metallic egg, over the house across the street," Albert remembered.

"Everyone started shouting that it was the Americans! I ran across the yard, following it. I stood right under it, looking at it. All of a sudden, it was like I snapped awake and it was gone. It was very late, and I was surprised that my parents hadn't been looking for me. I just went into the house and went to sleep. I have no idea how long I was out there."

Albert's Weirdest Cases

"Some of the most interesting cases are when people report different types of humanoids together," Albert said. "I remember a case from November 1973, in France."

This case, which took place between Mairiuex and Maubeuge Nord on November 26, 1973, at about 1 a.m., points up the frequent association between cryptids, particularly humanoids, and UFOs.

"Some people were sitting at the edge of a village, and they saw an object land in a nearby snowy field," Albert said. "A hatch opened, and several short humanoids with slightly large heads came out. After that, two tall humanoids with blond hair, and wearing silver-colored suits, came out. A few minutes later, something else came out."

The description of this final arrival matches none other than Bigfoot.

"They said it resembled a large ape or Bigfoot-type creature. It stood next to the craft the whole time."

According to the witnesses, the object was about 50 feet wide and about 100 yards away from them. Altogether, six beings emerged from the craft. The small humanoids were about four feet tall, and they supposedly had protruding eyes with conspicuous whites, a nose like two holes, bulging cheeks and mouths like slits. They had very long arms and were dressed in tightly-fitting suits of some metallic material.

Each carried a dark box, about six inches long, with what looked like a screen on the top. They walked slowly and stiffly, looking around as if searching for something.

Could they have been mechanical or biomechanical?

According to the witnesses, these short humanoids approached the road until they were about 50 feet away.

The two taller humanoids, whose blond hair was shoulder-length, were closer to the craft. The big, dark, hairy figure with dangling arms just stood by the craft, looking like Bigfoot.

Suddenly, the small humanoids approached the car. The woman screamed and jumped out, running to her own car and heading for the hills. That apparently startled their new friends, who turned and ran back to the craft with great speed, almost seeming to glide over the ground. The Big Guy was the first back into the craft, followed quickly by the five others.

According to the remaining witness, the craft lit up brightly, then rose about

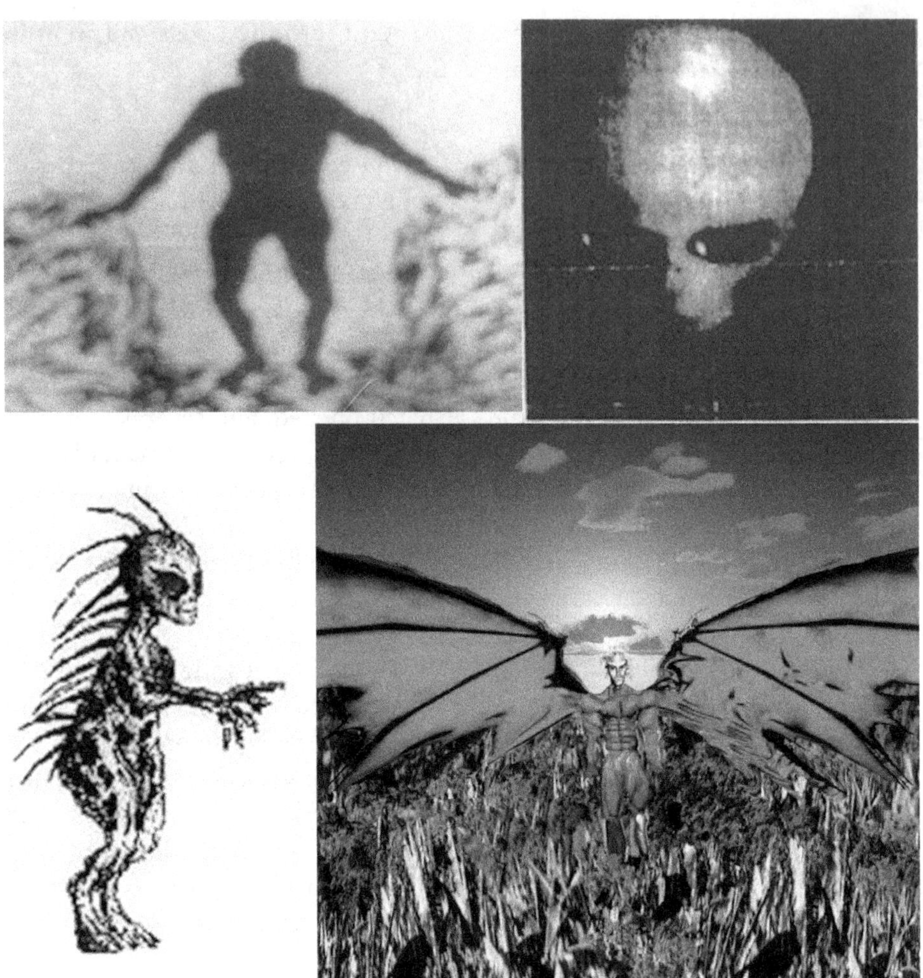

Some humanoid entities from the graphics collection of Albert Rosales. Clockwise from upper left: The image of the dark ape-like entity is from an uncredited photo of an Almasty, possibly from the Caucasus region of Russia. An enitity reported near Baker, California, in 1993. Image of a "Red Angel" reported to Albert in 1995 by a witness in Uganda. Finally, a sketch based on an eyewitness description of a chupacabra in Texas, nothing like the inbred, dog-coyote hybrids that are theorized as explanations. *Images Courtesy Albert Rosales.*

30 feet. It shot off toward the west, flashing orange, white, blue and red before disappearing. The next day, a woman and her children from a nearby house found unusual tracks in the snow.

"Different types of creatures appearing together like this are more common than you might think," Albert stated.

"What if you encounter a humanoid and it tries to gives you a message?" Ben Eno asked.

"I would just wait and see," Albert advised. "I wouldn't attempt to approach it or shine a light because that could be interpreted as aggression. I'd let them do whatever they want to do. I wouldn't initiate it."

Paul asked, "in what percentage of cases does a humanoid try to communicate?"

"More than I originally thought," Albert replied. "I'd say that in 40 percent of cases, there's an attempt at communication. That can range from verbal speech, telepathic communication, hand signals…all types. They even offer invitations to go with them."

We found that a little disconcerting. Albert continued.

"One witness said he asked how long he'd be gone. 'We'll bring you back in two months' was the answer. The guy refused."

We repeated one of our mottos: "Nothing in the paranormal is what it appears to be," and warned experiencers to be very careful. The parasites we talk about in other books are among the great mimics of Nature: They can appear to be aliens, humanoids, the ghosts of loved ones, and just about anything else. And the nature of the phenomena often change as soon as people figure that out, which they seldom do. We've seen confirmation of all this when working on crossover phenomena with some of the big names in UFO studies.

Parasites don't tell the truth. This is brought home in ancient legends of "the trickster," and Native American experiences with "skinwalkers."

The Flying Humanoids

While it might sound like a circus act, the flying humanoids, whether birdmen or human-like entities who appear to fly with the greatest of ease using machinery, are relatively common and can even be quite frightening.

"Flying humanoids are very popular lately," Albert said. "There have been many reports, especially from Mexico in 2009, when there were a slew of incidents."

There was another from California in January 2010, when people reported a man-like being in a metallic suit, flying horizontally – without wings.

"Definitely, some of these reports are hoaxes," said Albert. "This can be easy to hoax with balloons. On the other hand, a balloon doesn't make a level flight."

A Real Bruhaha in Mexico

Then there were the *bruha* (witch) sightings in the area of Monterrey, capital of Nuevo Leon state, in northeast Mexico, in the early 2000s. In one video, a figure wearing what appears to be a pointed hat walks along a ridge, then, at the edge of a cliff, just keeps walking, floating to the next ridge.

A related video can be seen on YouTube™ at https://www.youtube.com/watch?v=CeGkjIMzsVs.

In 2004, a young police officer in the same area saw something he interpreted as a *bruha* in a tree. It flew down and landed in front of his police car, frightening the daylights out of him.

Multiple Witnesses in St. Louis

Just before our July 29, 2012, *Behind the Paranormal* broadcast, Albert received an e-mail from a woman outside St. Louis, reporting a flying humanoid that had been seen only a few days before, on July 23.

"It was a Monday evening, and the family saw, flying over their house, a creature with huge, bat-like wings and the body of a human. It was light enough so they could see it clearly," said Albert. "They were adamant that it wasn't a kite or an aircraft."

Can anyone say "Mothman"?

"I can't keep up with the reports," Albert said.

Separating Fact from Fancy

"There are so many reports. It's almost impossible to tell, especially with cases from long ago or far away," commented Albert Rosales.

"If you get a local case where I can go myself and talk to the witness.... You can't believe everything they tell you or everything you read. I just try to catalog everything. Most of the time you can tell when someone is telling the truth or making up stories."

Paul meets the fairies – almost

If any humanoids can be said to blur the boundaries of reality, it's fairies. Fairies? Seriously?

In May 1984, just outside San Juan, Puerto Rico, it might be said that Paul Eno had a run-in with the "fair folk." On the suggestion of a local resident with whom he'd served in the U.S. Coast Guard, Paul visited a 40-ish couple in their lovely home in the hill country south of Puerto Rico's capital. He was a banker, she was a real estate agent, and they had three children, ages 9, 11 and 14.

"These were well-educated, professional people who spoke much better English than I spoke Spanish," Paul recalled.

"They were not bumpkins. But they were adamant that, each Saturday morning after breakfast, they would leave beer and fruit on the kitchen counter, then take their children for a walk for exactly one hour. When they returned, the entire house would be cleaned, and even the breakfast dishes would be washed and put away. They were convinced that this was being done by fairies!"

When Paul asked if anyone in the family had actually seen these fairies, the answer was a unanimous "yes"!

Both parents and all three children claimed they had seen small, glowing figures or orbs flitting about from time to time, especially in the winter, and apparently looking in their windows at night.

Asked how this convenient arrangement between the family and the wee sprites had come about, Paul was told that it was a gradual development.

"We had a party on a Saturday evening three years ago," the man explained. "It was late and we cleaned up as best we could, but we forgot to put away some beer and fruit. When we got up, the beer and fruit were gone, and the kitchen was spotless."

After that, the family gradually got the message that whatever it was liked to help with the housework, but that they didn't want to be seen doing it. So the Saturday walk developed.

Since the next day was Saturday, Paul returned early in the morning, setting up four cameras with trip wires in the kitchen. Then he took a very pleasant, one-hour walk with the family.

"Unfortunately, when we returned, neither the kitchen nor the rest of the house had been touched. Mom and Dad were irate, and blamed me. I thought I was going to have to clean the house!'

Why did Paul believe the story at all?

"I'd already been researching the paranormal for nearly 14 years, and I was pretty good at telling bovine fecal matter when I heard it. These people were dead serious and very sincere."

The Repeaters

People who have regular contact with humanoids, whether they be aliens, Bigfoot or fairies, like our friends in Puerto Rico, are known as "repeaters," according to Albert Rosales.

"It's actually quite common for people to have repeated encounters with the same or different entities," he said.

Albert said that he sometimes received reports of creatures that sound like fairies. One incident took place in June 2010, and came from the Ohio shore of Lake Erie.

"A man was walking his dog along the lake, but the dog was acting erratically," Albert said. "When they got back to their house, the dog was looking at the sky, and then they heard a noise in the woods. Suddenly he saw a peculiar, small, winged creature flying down across the front of house, with wings about three inches across. Like a fairy.

Ben spoke up.

"I think it's the word 'fairy' that invites disbelief because of its cartoon connotations. It doesn't mean that the human race hasn't grown up alongside a race of beings that we've enshrined in our folklore."

Fairies are one thing. But 'pukwudgies'?

One of the major paranormal flap areas we've investigated since 2010 is the "Bridgewater Triangle" in Massachusetts, not far from where we live. The heart of the triangle is the 5,441-acre Freetown-Fall River State Forest, which includes the 227-acre Watuppa Reservation, which belongs to the Wampanoag Nation, and is sacred land where annual tribal meetings are held.

One creature from Wampanoag folklore is the pukwudgie (probably derived from the Algonquian word *pukwudjeedj*. They are little humanoids, two to three feet tall, usually with large noses, ears and hands. Their skin is commonly described as gray, and it sometimes glows.

The Copicut Reservoir Beings

By 2016, we had already collected hundreds of reports of strange doings in the Bridgewater Triangle, and we'd talked with many eyewitnesses to odd events there, two of whom were police officers. Incidents involved Bigfoot, UFOs, giant birds, out-of-place panthers and other big cats, ghost phenomena, time slips…and what are known in the area as pukwudgies.

"I was walking my dog, Bingo, (a border collie), on the Sunday evening of May 17, 2015," one witness told Paul. "We were on a dirt road just north of the Copicut Reservoir. It was about 8 o'clock and just getting dark, and I was getting ready to turn around and head home."

Suddenly, Bingo started to whine. He was staring into the thick brush.

"As God is my witness, there was a little man standing there, no more than two feet high!" he told Paul. "My blood ran cold, and the hair on the back of my neck stood up! I knew I wasn't crazy because Bingo saw him too."

He described the small figure as "pale-faced" and wearing non-descript brown cloths.

"He had a smirk on his face, and he started gesturing for me to go with him into the woods. I was petrified, Bingo was whining and backing off, so I backed off too."

Suddenly, the small figure disappeared into the brush as if he'd never been there.

"We high-tailed it back to the car, and we've never been back there!"

Paul & Ben photograph…what?

A bit less than five years before this incident, on July 30, 2010, we headed for the Freetown-Fall River State Forest to do some exploring. That day alone convinced us that we should add the Bridgewater Triangle to our rapidly growing bag of paranormal flap areas.

Our own possible encounter with little people took place at or near the same

What appear to be small, humanoid figures appear in photos taken by the authors in the Bridgewater Triangle of Massachusetts in 2010. *Photos by Paul Eno.*

A common conception of a wood goblin, tree goblin (or pukwudgie?) from European folklore.
Kobzev Dmitry/Shutterstock

spot where our eyewitness and Bingo the dog would meet their pukwudgie.

"We stopped at a lovely spot at the northern end of the reservoir, just to get out of our Jeep and admire the view," Paul recalled. "But as soon as we stepped into the clearing, we had the strong feeling we were being watched."

On a hunch, Paul snapped a series of random photos. What showed up can be seen on the previous page. There appears to be a small human figure dressed in furs, and a head with a monk-like cowl.

"I did intelligence photography in the military," Paul said. "I realize that photos taken in the woods can be problematic. The interplay of sun and leaves can make you see almost anything."

What immediately drew Paul's attention, however, were the flesh tones.

"In this latitude, you almost never see that in nature except for certain fungi, and there were no fungi when I took these photos."

There are many other stories of the "puks," most of them unpleasant.

"We might be dealing with a form of parasite, or at least a trickster-being here," Paul suggested.

Folklorist, professor and expert on Native American traditions Dr. Wahabah Hadia al Mu'id (Page 109) appeared on *Behind the Paranormal* to fill us in on, among other things, pukwudgies.

"Sources have told me that the tree-knockings people usually associate with

The Monster Hunters

Dr. Wahabah Hadia al Mu'id

Wahabah Hadia al Mu'id

Wahabah has been involved in paranormal research for about 40 years. She holds a master's degree in religious studies and a doctorate in American cultural studies. Her thesis and dissertation covered different aspects of the UFO contact and abduction experiences in the United States, and she has written articles in a number of academic publications.

She has taught in virtually every educational setting, and now acts as a consultant for Bigfoot Researchers of the Hudson Valley (New York) and co-hosts the *Church of Mabus* podcast for UFO Paranormal Radio Network.

Also an experiencer, Wahabah is a master teacher, initiator, minister and dervish healer in the Western Sufi Order: Sufi Movement International. She teaches at Dutchess Community College in Poughkeepsie, New York.

She appeared on *Behind the Paranormal with Paul & Ben Eno* on October 30, 2016, discussing cultural variations in paranormal experiences.

Bigfoot are actually the *pukwudjeedj*, who live in trees. It's a way they use to signal to each other," Wahabah told us.

Paul pointed out that humans, at least in the Bridgewater Triangle, don't have a very good track record with the pukwudgies.

"According to the native tradition, there are many different types of little people. Some are oriented toward people and some are not," Wahabah replied.

"The important thing to understand is that they aren't here for us. They have their own existence. This is why the natives consider it important to establish a relationship with them."

It's important for all creatures to live in harmony, even with pukwudgies.

"When you don't do that, there might be some *pukwudjeedj* that decide they're going to mess with us."

Mermaids

Once we get past pukwudgies, we certainly ought to be able to deal with mermaids.

Sailors over the centuries have actually reported creatures much like these. Ancient sailors believed stories of the "sirens," mermaids whose singing would lure ships toward the rocks. More modern sailors might misinterpret seals seen on rocks. Original art by Karin Mansberg.

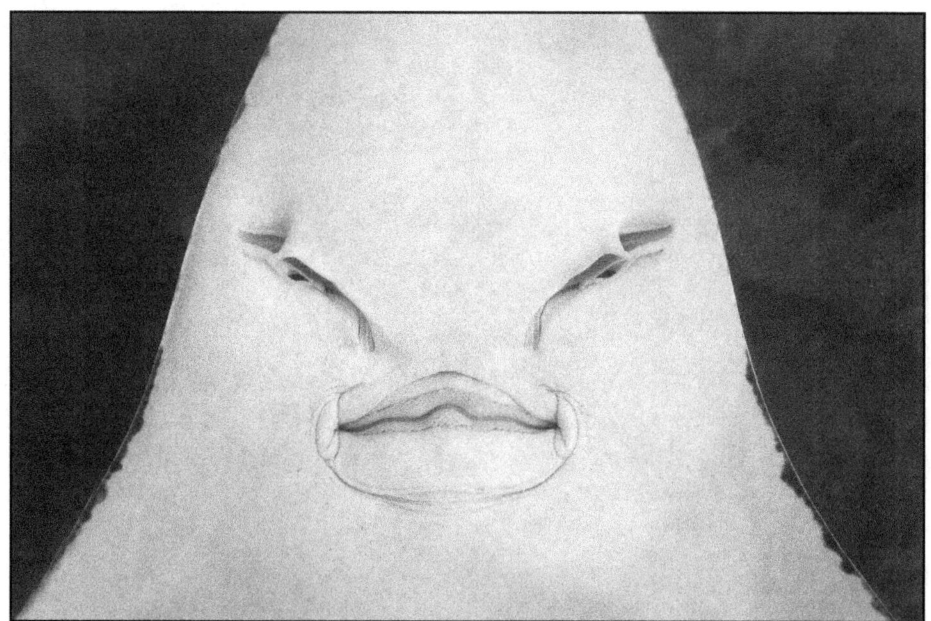

One theory for mermaid sightings is that some experiencers are actually seeing the guitar fish. If they were to catch sight of its underside from a certain distance, they would see this "face." The "eyes" are actually gills. *saiko3p/Shutterstock*

In July 2012, just before our weekly CBS Radio broadcast, the National Oceanic and Atmospheric Administration (NOAA) published a post on their "Ocean Facts" newsfeed entitled "No Evidence of Aquatic Humanoids Has Ever Been Found." The intent was to debunk claims of mermaid sightings, which were on the rise at the time.

"I guess that if the government denies something, there must be something to it," quipped humanoid chronicler Albert Rosales, who was back on the show.

In fact, there had been mermaid sightings in South Africa, Israel and Europe throughout the early 2000s, even in rivers and lakes.

In 2009, the city council of Kiryat Yam, on the Israeli coast near Haifa, offered a $1 million reward for proof of the existence of the mermaids tourists had reported seeing. Of course, this was certainly a ploy to boost tourism in the area, a popular vacation spot.

According to *The Jerusalem Post*, "mermaid fever" was gripping the area.

"Many people are telling us they are sure they've seen a mermaid, and they are all independent of each other," city council spokesman Natti Zilberman told Sky News.

"The nautical nymph is only seen in the evening at sunset, according to media reports, drawing crowds of people with cameras, hoping for a glimpse," *The Post* reported.

Cute, perhaps, but not pretty, one can see how the manatee, or sea cow, could be mistaken for a mermaid at a distance. *Andrea Izzotti/Shutterstock*

Witnesses said the creature or creatures were "half girl, half fish" and were "jumping like a dolphin."

"It does all kinds of tricks, then disappears," Zilberman was quoted as saying.

A Worldwide Phenomenon

Mermaids or merpeople seem to be a universal phenomenon, with sightings in both salt and fresh water. Albert Rosales mentioned the work of Zimbabwe researcher Cynthia Hind, who has documented sightings all over Africa, and in Europe and Russia.

In a South Africa case in 1991, the partial remains of an unknown humanoid were found in the stomach of a great white shark. The body had hands and a human-like skull. There was speculation that a stingray barb found stuck in the shark's jaw might have been used as a weapon by the humanoid.

"I think they're a species that might have developed alongside our own ancestors," Albert suggested. "We have to assume that a certain percentage of sightings are legitimate."

Even Christopher Columbus reported mermaids, in January 1493, Albert pointed out.

"They were probably manatees, which were not known in Europe. These animals are believed responsible for many mermaid sightings," he said. "There are always misidentifications."

Not all sightings are of creatures in the water.

"Some reports are from on shore. Witnesses have seen the (humanoid) details, and it's not a fish or other aquatic animal."

Explorer Henry Hudson had a mermaid sighting in June 1608, while he was near Russia, hunting for the Northwest Passage.

"Hudson described her in detail. The top half was that of a woman, with long black hair, and she had a speckled, porpoise-like tail. It sounds like something out of a children's book!" Albert said.

"The sea is so vast, and we know very little about it. Many parts are unexplored, so there certainly could be an aquatic humanoid species that has lived alongside us. It's certainly possible."

On the other hand, a number of aquatic animals could be mistaken for mermaids. These include manatees (sea cows), seals and guitar fish.

Asked if there has ever been communication between merpeople and those who encounter them, Albert said he had heard reports.

"There are reports from the 1800s and before, especially from the U.K. Supposedly, mermaids were captured, but they were never able to communicate. They either died or escaped."

A Merboy?

Albert shared an odd report from Puerto Rico.

"In 1992, a man and his son were alone on a beach, and they described a little boy who came out of the water. He was human in appearance. He draw some signs on the sand, made some hand signals, then disappeared back into the water."

More Aquatic Humanoids

Merpeople aren't the only aquatic humanoids reported, according to Albert.

"After Hurricane Floyd struck the coast of Florida in 1999, a diver reported what looked like an amphibian humanoid. It had appendages like arms, but with claws. It had long, flowing hair and smooth skin, but it was horrible in appearance."

The diver pushed it away when it came near him, and said that he felt strongly that it wanted to harm him.

"That's one of the few cases I know of where the witness felt threatened," Albert stated.

"How many cases have multiple witnesses?" Paul asked.

"In the Israeli case and some of the older British cases, there have been many witnesses. The more modern cases tend to have fewer witnesses," Albert replied.

He related a September 2007 case from Quistococha Lake, in Iquitos, Peru.

"There was a mermaid-like entity seen by 20 students. They described her as a fish-tailed woman in the middle of the lake, frolicking in the water. She dove when she saw that she was being observed."

Ben noted that there are cave paintings of people with fishtails, and some with humans throwing spears at them.

"There's a Babylonian scroll that suggests their civilization was started by a fish-like humanoid that came out of the water," said Albert.

This was none other than Oannes, the amphibious god who taught humans wisdom, according to the Babylonians.

During the show, a listener asked if merpeople could actually be spirits. Albert was doubtful.

"I've never thought of it like that. I've never heard of them being compared with spirits."

Humanoids in Cave Paintings

Spirits or not, humanoids, complete with bulging eyes and features that, to us, would make them look like Hollywood space aliens, turn up in 30,000- to 40,000-year-old cave paintings, indicating that strange humanoid beings of some kind were known to our remote ancestors.

At the Wandjina Overhang in the Kimberly Region of Western Australia are these humanoid figures. Wandjina is an aboriginal word for creator spirit. *Courtesy Australian Tourism Commission*

The Butterfly People of Joplin

On May 22, 2011, Joplin, Missouri was devastated by an EF-5 tornado. According to a number of people, especially children, who nearly lost their lives, the first responders weren't limited to police, firefighters and emergency medical technicians.

The issue came up on our first open-line show of 2017, and it brought to mind suggestions by Wahabah Hadia al Mu'id that people interpret, and even experience, paranormal phenomena in general, and cryptids in particular, from the viewpoints of their own cultures.

Within a few days of the disaster in Joplin, children began telling adults about "butterfly people" they had seen during and after the storm and who had, in some cases, saved their lives.

There were many stories. Most commonly, a child would see a butterfly person, a humanoid but with colorful wings, hovering above them and their adult guardians as the tornado approached. Some children thought they were angels. Others talked about an "indescribable presence."

Whatever they were, the children and adults always emerged unharmed, in most cases from impossibly dangerous situations when it came to the storm.

So moved were the people of Joplin that they commissioned mural artist Dave Loewenstein, who worked with 15 local artists and up to 200 people, including many children, who volunteered to help by submitting drawings. The mural, including renditions of the butterfly people, now adorns the side of the Dixie Printing Building in Joplin.

Perhaps this is one more clue in our contention that, despite parasites and scary cryptids, the ultimate message of the paranormal is one of unity and love.

As heard on

CBS Radio August 22, 2010
WOON 1240 Radio – February 2, 2015

"It was like being in the last scene of the 1929 movie Dracula, with Lon Chaney, where the torch-bearing townspeople attack the castle."

That was Paul Eno's thought as he charged across a moor in North Devon, England's, magnificent Exmoor National Park in March 1989, accompanied by two local police officers and four sheep farmers armed with shutguns.

"He must be in there!" shouted one farmer, as they headed toward a small stand of trees, about an acre in size.

"The farmer might have been right. As we approached the trees, we all heard something large charge through the underbrush in the opposite direction. We neither saw it nor heard it again that day," Paul recalled.

The four farmers claimed they had been losing sheep at a rate of two to three a month that year, and the culprit, they believed, was none other than the "Black Beast of Exmoor." Paul interviewed 18 farmers in North Devon that week, all of whom had lost livestock, and eight of whom had actually seen the "beast," a black panther or mountain lion that had no business being in the British Isles. One farmer, just outside the village of Molland, had seen two of them together, describing them both as "pot-bellied."

"I met only one skeptic, a pub owner who was convinced that the farmers were running an insurance scam," Paul noted.

The Royal Marines evidently weren't so skeptical. Six years before Paul was there, and in response to all the sheep kills, the British Government decided to kill two beasts with one stone, as it were.

"This was partly as a sniper-training exercise, and partly a way to find if there

A picture of what appears to be a black panther. This was taken on the moors of North Devon, England, during the Black Beast of Exmoor frenzy in the 1980s, by researcher Nigel Brierly, who sent it to Paul Eno in 1989. *Photo courtesy Nigel Brierly*

really was a predator on the loose," Paul's friend Nigel Brierly, a local big-cat researcher, told him at the time.

"The Marines were using night-vision scopes. Several of them saw the animal, but they couldn't get a clear shot," added Nigel, whose goal was to eventually trap one of the cats. As far as we know, he never did.

After the Marines left, things only got worse. By the time Paul got there, the "beast" was blamed for well over 150 sheep deaths, and the killing of several wild moor ponies. People were beginning to worry about their small children.

Paul didn't see any beasts that week, but he did see telltale tracks, scat with huge claw marks around it, and sheep kills.

"It was clear that the sheep had been killed, and the meat licked out from the bones, as a large cat would do," he said. "These didn't have any appearance of having been killed by a dog."

Richard Freeman of the Centre for Fortean Zoology, also a friend of Nigel Brierly, appeared on *Behind the Paranormal with Paul & Ben Eno* to share his information.

"In the spring of 2011, on the outskirts of Exeter in Devon, in a field in broad daylight, there was a black puma, bold as brass," Richard told us. "It was standing by a tree and was the size of an Alsatian dog."

Richard said that not much had changed since Paul's 1989 beast hunt.

"We still see the sheep kills, and there are more and more reports. There seems to be a population of these cats throughout the country. People are concerned for their children," Richard said.

There have been hundreds of witnesses, not only to the Beast of Exmoor but to many other out-of-place big cats in Britain, including the Cotswolds Big Cat and the Beast of Bodmin Moor. There are many photos, and several big cats have actually been captured in Britain or killed by motor vehicles.

While Paul and Richard's friend Nigel might have been unsuccessful with his trap, Scottish farmer Ted Noble wasn't. In 1980, he captured Felicity the Puma, who ended up in the Inverness Zoo. When she died, Felicity ended up stuffed, in the Inverness Museum, where she can be seen today.

One Step Ahead of the Law

There might be a very practical reason why there have been so many big cats seen in Britain since the 1970s.

"In that decade, it became cool to buy exotic big cats as pets," explained paranormal researcher and monster hunter *extraordinaire* Nick Redfern. "At the time, there was no government legislation on this. You could go out and buy a leopard or mountain lion and just keep it in your back garden with no problem."

All that changed in 1976, when the British Parliament passed the Dangerous Wild Animals Act.

"Owners had to prove they could keep the animal safely, that it couldn't escape, and then they had to get an expensive license. If they couldn't do that, they had to give their animals to zoos," Nick said.

"Many people just took their animals to the woods or fields, then let them go in twos or threes. Certainly, some of them bred, and the reports we hear now are probably the third or fourth generation of cats."

That's precisely the conclusion Paul Eno arrived at while he was chasing these cats around the English West Country in 1989. But not so fast....

"What makes it more puzzling is that we even have reports of these big cats from the 1920s, 1930s, all the way back to the 1600s," Nick said. "Maybe these big cats have been in Britain longer than many people realize."

It's possible that explorers brought back the ancestors of at least some of these cats centuries ago. Or they might even be traceable to the Romans, nearly 2,000 years ago.

"The Romans were in Britain for 300 years, and they liked to keep lions as mascots. Some might have escaped and been breeding all this time, and there are plenty of rabbits and deer for them to eat," Nick suggested.

From Old England to New England

Whether we call them panthers, pumas, mountain lions, cougars or just "big cats," these beasts haven't been indigenous to Britain (at least not officially) for a formidable number of centuries. But there's no denying that they still thrive in the mountains of North America, primarily in the West.

In New England, there hasn't been an official big-cat sighting since the one in Barnard, Vermont, in 1881. As a matter of fact, the eastern panther has been listed as extinct. Nevertheless, unofficial sightings of it and other anomalous cats, up to 40 a year, have been reported to local conservation officials over the past three decades.

New England consists of the six small states (small for America, at least) in the extreme northeast corner of the United States, which figure prominently in history books of the colonial and revolutionary periods: Connecticut, Rhode Island, Massachusetts, Vermont, New Hampshire and Maine. Outside of urban areas such as Boston, Providence and Hartford, there are many surprisingly isolated tracts, especially in northern New England. Still, much of southern New England is well populated, with broad residential development, and the appearance of big cats here is surprising to say the least.

Panthers, or "catamounts" as they traditionally are known in New England, once lived throughout the forests of North America. As European settlers moved in during the 17th century and the human population expanded, big cats and other wilderness species headed for "greener pastures," or disappeared entirely from this part of the continent.

Since about 1980, however, it seems to have dawned on several of these species that humans may not make such bad neighbors after all, primarily because of the latters' wasteful habits and well-laden rubbish bins. In the past few decades, rural homeowners throughout New England have reported an increase in coyotes, black bear, moose and even wolves, which forage routinely in some backyards and nearby fields. Officials have had to warn transplanted city dwellers not to feed them.

Contributing to this renewal are strict laws protecting endangered species and severe restrictions on hunting in many areas, all accompanied by an amazing rise in the deer population because of the predators' lengthy absence.

We live in a belt of suburban communities and old mill towns within 35 miles of Boston, and hardly a month goes by when one of our neighbors doesn't lose a cat or dog to one of the coyotes that have multiplied in our region. They were unheard of here before 1980, but with deer so numerous, it's not surprising that predators are on the increase too.

At night, we sometimes hear coyotes yipping in the woods on the hill behind our northern Rhode Island home.

Into this new environmental picture strides the big cat. And while there is no official acknowledgement of his return to New England, there is little doubt that return he has, and on occasion in a hybrid form that equals any of the odd, pseudo-domestic sheep killers of the British moors.

The reports of both normal and hybrid animals are as varied as the places from which they come. Colors range from grey and reddish to dark brown, yellowish or tawny. A few are reported as solid black. Length, *not* including the tail, has been reported at up to an astounding seven feet.

The Peduzzi Sighting, 1946

In his book *Green Mountain Ghosts, Ghouls and Unsolved Mysteries*, our friend Joseph Citro describes Marian Harpan Peduzzi's encounter with a black panther on a dirt road in Berlin, Vermont, in 1946. Peduzzi was walking home at about 4 p.m. one afternoon when she noticed what she thought was a black Labrador retriever. She quickly realized, however, that it was a large cat, about 300 feet away.

Shocked, the woman sprinted to the nearby home of a friend, who later confirmed the sighting. With the two women watching, the panther got up and ran toward the house, coming within 25 feet of them before it veered off into the woods. They later described the cat as roughly four feet long, with a long tail and glossy black fur.

On the Appalachian Trail

During the summer of 1979, David Czaja reported a big-cat encounter while hiking on the Appalachian Trail (a magnificent, 2,000-mile footpath that runs through the mountains from Maine to Georgia). He was in Salisbury, Connecticut.

"I encountered a mountain lion," Mr. Czaja reported. "Several others in my group saw it as well. It was initially 30 to 40 feet away on the trail, then ran another 40 to 50 feet away before bounding into the brush, and was gone," he said.

"Since then, I have maintained an interest in the possibility of mountain lions in Connecticut, and kept an informal listing of sightings through the '80s and '90s. Cats have been seen by those I consider to be reliable sources throughout north-western as well as central Connecticut."

He noted that sightings near suburban areas tend to be near public reservoirs surrounded by ledges and other rough terrain, and that are connected with other rural or wilderness areas. Mr. Czaja has documented other sightings near the beautiful Barkhamsted Reservoir in East Hartland, Connecticut.

"All the sightings I'm aware of include comments on the tail, which a friend and two-time cat-sighting veteran calls an appendage in itself," Mr. Czaja commented.

The Mansfield Mystery Cat

A little more than three years after Paul Eno's Beast of Exmoor expedition, he received an unexpected telephone call from the Massachusetts Environmental Police.

"Somebody here read something you wrote about that lion in England," declared the voice on the line. "People claim they have one in Mansfield. What do we do about it?"

Taken aback, all Paul could say was, "If it's really there, try not to let it breed!"

Mansfield, Massachusetts, is about 20 miles from where Paul lived in Rhode Island, so he was delighted, astonished and frantic to find out more.

The media soon dubbed the culprit the "Mansfield Mystery Cat," and there were over 20 reports of a "large, light-tan cat the size of a Great Dane" on the loose. Paul found that local authorities took the matter lightly, until someone got a rather decent videotape of the huge housecat look-alike calmly washing its paws next to a field of tall grass, which gave the animal an alarming scale. From the tape, one state biologist estimated to Paul that the cat could have been nearly five feet long, minus the tail, and weighed over 200 lbs.

Mansfield Fire Chief Edward Sliney told Paul that he had laughed at reports of the cat until he saw it himself, across the road from his own house! The authorities then started taking reports very seriously.

Interestingly, Mansfield is near the heart of the Bridgewater Triangle and the Hockomock Swamp Management Area, a 200 square-mile wilderness with a history of bizarre happenings that reaches back long before European settlement. Giant cats, Bigfoot-like creatures, giant snakes, oversized birds and even UFOs are but a few of the tamer phenomena supposedly witnessed in this flap area over the centuries.

During the late 1970s, reports flooded the local police department of a massive canine, much bigger than any normal dog, responsible for killing ponies and terrorizing humans on dark roads. During the same decade, local police reportedly had a most unpleasant encounter with Bigfoot, which allegedly picked up the back of one of the police cars, then dropped it with an unfortunate officer still inside.

Later in 1993, a few months after the Mansfield Mystery Cat seemed to have moved on, two reports of similar sightings came from Lincoln Woods State Park in Rhode Island, not many miles from the Eno door. While Mansfield is largely rural, Lincoln is virtually in the shadow of Providence, the state capital and a port city of over 160,000 people.

Other sightings in the past few years have come from elsewhere in Rhode Island, from Vermont and New Hampshire, and several from Maine.

Rattled Raccoons

Our colleague Shane Sirois had his own up-close and dramatic experience with a mountain lion on his property in New Hampshire in 2016.

"I was up late, watching pay-per-view boxing. It was close to 1 a.m. when I heard a loud, screaming roar," Shane told us.

Peering out his glass-paneled back door, he saw two raccoons with their backs hunched up.

"They were hopping around with their jaws quivering. I then noticed a large silhouette to the left, in the darkness."

The backyard light was blocked by a corner of the house. The raccoons were illuminated, but the large animal wasn't. Shane, however, is fearless.

"I opened the door slowly when this thing made another loud, screaming roar. It was, without a doubt, the roar of a mountain lion. This made the raccoons back up and, when they did, the mountain lion moved forward into the light. I saw it! It was very large," Shane said.

"Some people confuse bobcats with mountain lions. I know the difference. This was large, with a long tail."

After the mountain lion moved forward, the raccoons bolted.

"There's a chainlink fence over six feet tall. It had a small opening in one spot, where animals dug in order to come through from the woods. The raccoons ran under the fence at that same spot. The mountain lion, being way too big to fit, jumped on top of the fence," Shane related.

"The raccoons, instead of taking off through the woods, decided to climb the nearest tree. As they were ascending, the mountain lion jumped from the fence onto the tree and grabbed a raccoon! The mountain lion was so heavy the tree snapped and fell into another tree."

The tree that snapped was a fully grown white birch. The surviving raccoon continued to climb from the birch onto the supporting tree, and all the way to the top.

"I went back in and finished watching boxing. I was up late, so I slept in the next morning, and got up about 9 a.m.," Shane recalled "I went outside with a cup of coffee to look at the snapped tree. The surviving raccoon was still bear-hugging the top of that tree. It looked completely traumatized. After a few hours, it finally made its way down. There's no doubt in my mind that mountain lions are back. I saw one," Shane concluded.

The Evidence

In nearly 40 years as a journalist and 50 as a connoisseur of the bizarre, Paul has found that eyewitnesses can be very reliable. Still, the best "witness" is physical evidence, and that we have in many of the New England sightings:

photographs, tracks, scat, and deer and livestock killed and eaten big-cat style, not to mention reliable eyewitness accounts like Shane's. A 1994 scat sample proved the presence of a family of catamounts -- a mother and two kittens -- in Craftsbury, Vermont. And in 1995, scientists used hair samples to document the presence of a mountain lion at Cape Elizabeth, Maine.

Nevertheless, to our knowledge, not one of these cats has been captured or shot in New England. And we haven't heard of one being struck by a car, though an unmistakable tail convinced Paul that one of these very beasts, seemingly a black panther about four feet long, ran across a road in front of his car on December 20, 1999, in Burrillville, Rhode Island, even as he was headed home to finish an article for a British magazine on this very subject.

Those who acknowledge that the cats are here say they could be transplanted western cougars or illegally purchased black panthers that have escaped or were released. Nevertheless, the number of annual sightings suggests a larger population of cats than officials have been willing to admit. Most wildlife biologists, particularly those who work for government agencies, insist that the eastern panther remains dead.

"I think that (one 1998 Smithfield, Rhode Island, witness) has a moderately high credibility," said Michael Lapisky, former deputy chief of wildlife resources for that state's Department of Environmental Management. "I think he did see something. But statistically, it's very, very unlikely that it's a wild animal. If you have the physical evidence that says cougar, I'm going to tell you it's probably an escaped pet."

Todd Lester, founder of the Eastern Cougar Resource Center, in West Virginia, told Paul that's just the response he'd expect from a government official.

"If they admitted they were here, they'd have to spend money to protect them," said Todd, one of dozens of researchers throughout the United States dedicated to proving the continued existence of the eastern panther.

The debate about existence and origins will continue, both in New England and Old England. After all, for the believer, no proof is required; for the unbeliever, no proof is sufficient.

No Pouch Potatoes Here

Out-of-place-animals, sometimes called "animal erratics," include far more than big cats. There are crazy kangaroos, too.

The American Midwest was the scene of a bizarre outbreak of the manic marsupials in the 1970s. The most sightings took place in Illinois and Indiana, very far from their native Australia. Nevertheless, they were seen by a number of reliable witnesses, including police officers. Strangely, no-one seemed able to catch one.

Belle Ciezak/Shutterstock

One of the first roo-human encounters took place on the morning of October 18, 1974, when surprised Chicago police received a call from a man who claimed there was a five-foot kangaroo in his backyard. Amused officers Leonard Ciagi and Michael Byrne were dispatched to the scene, only to find that the man was telling the truth. Even the cops couldn't capture the critter, however. They even tried to handcuff it, but the tough little *macropodida* punched and kicked the officers until they backed off.

When more police arrived, along with animal control personnel, the roo decided that retreat was the better part of valor, leaped over a fence and vanished. A delighted media dubbed the animal the "Chicago Hopper" as they reported sightings all over that city's northwestern suburbs the following week.

One would expect that any kangaroo found in America would be on the lam from some zoo or circus, but no-one reported any missing kangaroos.

In late October that year, kangaroos began turning up in Indiana, even while they were still appearing in Chicago. On November 2, three people saw a kangaroo in Plano, Indiana, and within half an hour another one was seen 50 miles away, on the outskirts of Chicago. The sightings continued in Indiana and Illinois until November 25, when the whole business stopped as suddenly as it had started.

By 1978, kangaroos were being reported in the Waukesha, Wisconsin, area. Researchers, including Loren Coleman (Page 9), got plaster casts of kangaroo tracks. Also in April of 1978, two men near Menominee Falls, Wisconsin, got a photo of a kangaroo they stumbled on in the woods. The following year, there were kangaroo sightings in Ontario and New Brunswick, Canada.

One of the more notable kangaroo flaps took place in the Tulsa, Oklahoma, area in 1981. In one case, a man walked into a coffee shop in Tulsa and said he'd nearly had an accident in his pickup truck while trying to avoid a kangaroo in the road. But in doing that, he'd struck and killed a second one. Sure enough, there was the dead roo in the back of his truck for all to see. The "all" included not only the coffee shop customers but two Oklahoma state cops. The man then drove off with the evidence.

One of the officers later said, "I wish I'd taken a picture."

The Kangaroo from Hell

Moving into deepest, darkest cryptozoology, residents of Hamburg, Arkansas, reported a kangaroo-like creature that terrorized the region in 1934. They said it looked like a kangaroo, but was huge and unlike anything they'd ever seen. One eyewitness was a local minister, the Rev. W. J. Hancock. He said it was "as fast as lightning...running and leaping across the fields."

While these sightings took place, something was killing and eating dogs, ducks and geese. Kangaroos, of course, are vegetarians. Bands of armed men from the area tracked the creature into the hills, but couldn't find it.

7 MONSTERS YOU NEVER HEARD OF

As heard on
CBS Radio – August 22, 2010, January 22, 2012
WOON 1240 Radio – September 6, 2010,
January 5, 2015, December 4, 2016

The Feathered Serpent. Goatman. The Owlman. *El Chupacabras*. The Batsquatch. The Flathead Lake Monster. Lizardman. So far in this book, we've only scratched the weird surface of the cryptid world, or worlds. In fact, the paranormal has always been entirely normal. The Native Americans knew this.

"Certainly one of the strangest legends is that of Quetzalcoatl (ket-zel co-at-tle), the "feathered serpent" or "plumed serpent," researcher Linda Godfrey pointed out during one of her appearances on *Behind the Paranormal with Paul & Ben Eno.*

"This Mesoamerican god can be found in several ancient South American cultures, sometimes under different names and with slight variations. He was known to the Aztecs and the Mayans, but what was he?" asked Linda.

To the Mayans, he was Kukulkán, and Ehecatl to the Huastecs of the Gulf Coast. The Quiché of Guatemala called him Gucumatz.

"Quetzalcoatl was a flying, serpentine being who bears a resemblance to dragons, early gods in China and old Sumerian civilizations," said Linda. "They go way, way back. They prefigure the thunderbird as described by the North American natives."

A highly placed spirit creature with feathers, Quetzalcoatl was generally described as of huge size, and was able to battle other supernatural creatures or to connect with human civilizations. And he was pretty important, regarded as the creator of the world and the one who governed wind and water. He was the patron of science, the arts and farming. He sometimes took human form.

Another humanoid, perhaps?

An image of Quetzalcoatl as seen at the Temple of the Feathered Serpent, Xochicalco, Mexico.
Byelikova Oksana/Shutterstock

Goatman Butts In

Nick Redfern told us about the Goatman of Lake Worth, Texas, also known as the Lake Worth Monster.

"It's a strange name. Sounds like some of the ancient Greek legends, a creature with cloven hoofs, horns and fur, but it looks human," Nick said. "It was first seen near Lake Worth in the 1960s. Local police took it very seriously, and the file is kept to this day at Lake Worth Police Department."

A number of local people reported a half-man, half-goat, with fur and scales, in July 1969. The local press reported that one man was terrified by the creature when it jumped out of a tree and landed on his car.

"People reported this weird creature running across roads and in the woods," Nick said. "Sightings went on for months, but trailed off around 1971. There are still sporadic reports."

The townspeople made the most of Goatman, however, and today there's an annual festival in his honor.

There are plenty of other goatmen, especially in North American urban legends, stories that people tell each other about odd or funny happenings, and that grow in the telling. But the sheer number of goatman reports since the 1950s does make us wonder.

Within the last 20 years, goatmen have been reported not only in Texas, but in Arkansas, Maryland, Kentucky, Wisconsin, Alabama, California, Indiana,

Michigan, Oregon, Texas and Washington, as well as in Canada, South Africa and many other countries.

The Maryland Goatman is one of several that have taken on a modern techno-twist. Rumor has it that he was genetically engineered at the Beltsville Agricultural Research Center, or that he was an unfortunate human bitten by a genetically modified goat. Regardless of his origin, he was a fright to many teenagers on lovers' lanes, and was said to be a danger to life and limb if one got too close to his lair. Several murders were popularly blamed on him.

The Greek God Pan certainly can be considered the prototypical goatman. Benign but moody, Pan, with the legs and horns of a goat, is honored as the guardian of fields, forests, sheep and shepherds, and the friendly companion of the nymphs. Among his people are the lusty satyrs, goatmen all.

Monkeying Around

Nick Redfern described one of the earliest creatures he himself investigated, near his hometown in England. It might belong in the Bigfoot chapter. Then again, it might not.

"I grew up near Birmingham, in central England, but well into the countryside," Nick told us. "There are towns and villages there that really haven't changed in 200 or 300 years, in some cases. There are lots of castles and old buildings."

Amid this otherwise quaint scene, there was a Bigfoot-like creature that haunted a bridge, at the hamlet of Ranton, Staffordshire. It was first reported in 1883 and was generally considered to be the ghost of an animal.

"It became known as the Man Monkey, but it was more spectral than the usual Bigfoot," Nick added. "It had glowing white eyes. A man chasing it on a horse was seen to ride right through it."

In 1879, a man and his horse supposedly were attacked by the Man Monkey, who seems to have a number of cousins around the world. In Ranton, however, the Man-Monkey hasn't been seen in many years.

El Chupacabras

Probably better known than most of the entities discussed in this chapter, *El Chupacabras* literally means "sucks goats" in Spanish. These little darlings have been described in many ways.

"Some say it's like a hairless monkey, with claws and fangs, and sometimes with a row of spikes down its back," Nick Redfern told us. "I've made a number of trips to Puerto Rico to hunt for *El Chupacabras*, and it's one of my favorite expeditions."

Some descriptions give the creature bat-like wings, along with the other characteristics. And it has been blamed for attacking cattle, particularly sheep and goats, not only in Puerto Rico but throughout Central America, up into the American Southwest, and as far north as Maine.

While creatures like *El Chupacabras* can be found in folklore, the first eyewitness sightings that were publicized in modern times took place in Puerto Rico in 1995. Eight sheep were found with three fang marks in their chests, and they were totally drained of blood.

"In Puerto Rico, I found reports that predate the term *El Chupacabras* by decades," Nick stated. "In 2004, I first interviewed a woman who lived high in the El Yunque rain forest. She described a creature she'd seen in the summer of 1975 or 1976."

Reports said that its blood-drained victims had only one puncture wound instead of the usual three.

In the 1980s, there were other reports of small-animal mutilations and blood-draining in Puerto Rico, according to Nick.

"I also heard about what local people called the Moca Vampire. That referred to mutilations and blood-draining that took place in northwestern Puerto Rico in the 1980s," he said.

Nick agreed wholeheartedly with us that "if you gain the trust of the locals, you can hear lots of stories. And those stories go way back."

Farther north, there's a variation on this critter, known as the Appalachian Chupacabra, which supposedly migrated to the East Coast of North America from Puerto Rico in the 1800s. First reports date from the 20th century, especially from our old paranormal stomping ground of West Virginia. There, hunters, hikers on the famed Appalachian Trail and other outdoorsy types reported finding wildlife with fang marks in their necks and drained of blood.

Others reported direct encounters, not with an individual Appalachian Chupacabra, but with an entire pack.

The Mongolian Death Worm

Richard Freeman is a trained zoologist, and a renowned British author and adventurer. When he joined us on *Behind the Paranormal*, one of our first questions was, "What's the weirdest cryptid you've ever hunted?"

"The weirdest has to be the Mongolian Death Worm," was Richard's immediate reply. "By the time these stories from the Gobi Desert nomads reach the West, they've grown into a creature worthy of doing battle with Dr. Who. It's two to five feet long, red, and can spit a corrosive acid. They can generate blasts of electricity that can kill a full-grown camel or human."

Richard traveled over 1,000 miles through the Gobi, an arid, half-million square-mile wilderness area shared by China and Mongolia. There, he interviewed nomads who claimed to have seen the Death Worm.

"It's a different animal altogether," Richard told us. "The electricity, or 'throwing lightning,' as they call it, is complete folklore, I'm sure. Most people describe a creature, usually around two feet long, as thick as a human arm. It's seen in the desert or slithering in and out of holes. People are absolutely terrified of it. They believe it's highly venomous and can spit."

Richard spoke with one man who had seen a death worm as a child.

"His whole family took their livestock and their yurt and moved out of the area. They were frightened to death!"

Richard suggests that the Death Worm might be a reptile of some kind, not a true worm.

"The Gobi is a very strange desert. It's not like the Sahara. Some of it is sand, and much of it is rock. Some of it looks like the surface of Mars or Mordor. Other parts are like a huge mirror, shiny and flat. And there are all sorts of mirages," Richard said.

"The Death Worm certainly could be an undiscovered species of sand boa or burrowing worm lizard," he added. "But I think the spitted poison is apocryphal. Similar stories are told about a species of sand boa in Somalia. Touch it and fall dead, they say. It's actually harmless."

Richard compared folk beliefs about the Death Worm to fear of salamanders and basilisks in medieval Europe.

A common description of the Mongolian Death Worm. belizar/Shutterstock

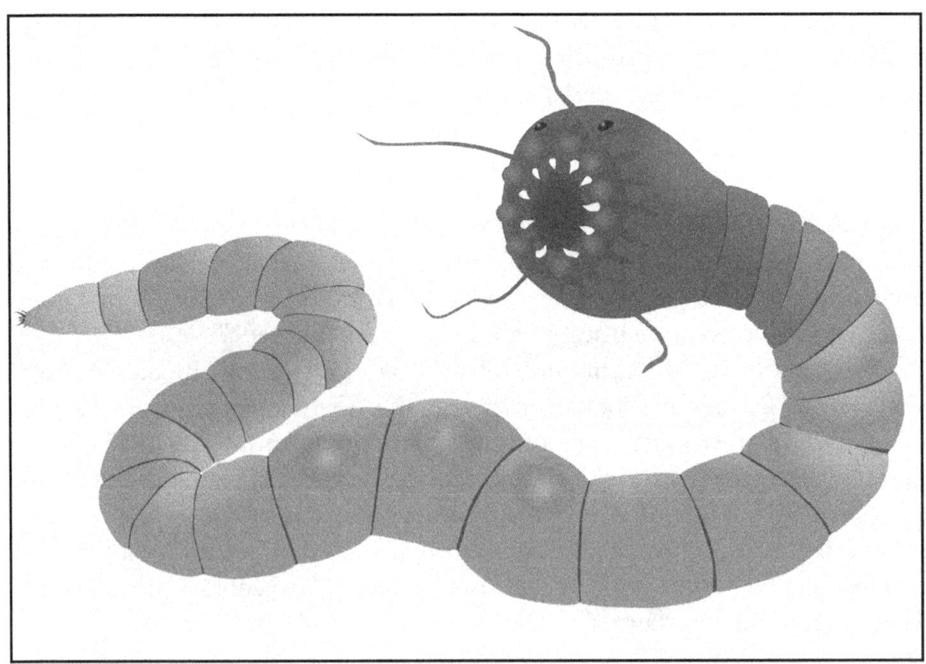

The Orang Pendek, as depicted by artist Karin Mansberg.

The Orang Pendek

The Orang Pendek is a small, Bigfoot-like creature that supposedly lives in the mountains and forests of the large Indonesian island of Sumatra. Many local people claim to have seen it, and Richard Freeman believes he has heard it.

"It has also been seen by Dutch colonists, western researchers, and travellers. I've seen tracks of the Orang Pendek, and heard it calling," Richard told us. "I've spoken with many people who've seen it. My good friend Dave Archer and a native guide both saw the Orang Pendek in 2009, from about 100 feet. It was frightened."

In the Bahasa Indonesian language, *Orang Pendek* literally means "short man" or "dwarf." Richard has tracked it on four different expeditions to Sumatra.

"They are solitary creatures," said Richard, who said he has hair samples.

"As a zoologist, I can say that its tracks are different from apes. As for the hair, this has been analyzed by different labs. Dr. Lars Thomas at the University of Copenhagen has concluded that it's related to the orangutan, but distinct from it," Richard stated.

"I have no doubt the Orang Pendek exists."

The Batsquatch of Tacoma

The Batsquatch could be a variation on Mothman, Bigfoot or both, said Linda Godfrey, who told us that she has personally investigated one sighting in Wisconsin. The first report, however, comes from Pierce County, Washington, near Tacoma, in April 1994.

A man was driving along when his pickup truck's engine suddenly died. This takes place when anything electrical runs into an electromagnetic pulse (EMP), which happens at the moment of a nuclear explosion -- or when there's a quick and violent breach of a parallel-world boundary or brane.

The creature that landed right in front of the truck, in full view of driver Brian Canfield, was humanoid, covered with blue fur, and was about nine feet tall, with bat-like wings 20 to 30 feet in diameter.

Reporter C.R. Roberts from the *Tacoma News Tribune* interviewed Canfield.

"'It looked like a huge, furry, wolf-like thing,' Canfield told him," Linda said. "He saw it descend from the sky and land about 30 feet down the road. It stirred up a huge cloud of dust when it landed."

The being stared at Canfield.

"Actually, the man said it looked confused and scared. It had yellow eye-shine like a canine, white teeth but no fangs, with a face like a wolf, and that strange blue fur. Finally, it unfolded its wings and flapped off, also in a cloud of dust," Linda said.

Canfield told Roberts: "It was standing there like it was resting. Staring at me like it didn't know what to think. I didn't feel threatened, I just felt out of place."

Did Canfield feel out of place because he was partially in the creature's parallel world? In any case, Roberts believed Canfield.

Other sightings of a similar creature have been reported near Akron, Ohio, and Mt. Shasta, California.

"With furry, humanoid bodies, glowing red eyes and bat-wings wider than a pickup truck, they seem to enjoy swooping at passing vehicles and pedestrians," Linda noted. "Reports are most numerous in the northwestern United States, but Batsquatch has been spied in rural Wisconsin, West Virginia, Pennsylvania and even downtown Chicago. Some researchers believe it's an unknown, giant bat species."

Descriptions of the Batsquatch remind us of the ancient Mesopotamian god Anzu. In Sumerian and Akkadian mythology, he was the divine storm-bird. Could human encounters with some Batsquatch-like creature have prompted legends of creatures like Anzu?
Zvereva Iana/Shutterstock

More imaginative people suggest that "its fly-bys are out-of-time appearances by a Sumerian demon-god named Pazuzu. Frankly, I don't know what it is," Linda said.

Interestingly, the Sumerians, with an odd history and even more mysterious origins (see the first chapter of the first book in this series, *Behind the Paranormal: Everything You Know is Wrong*, Schiffer Books, 2016), almost always depicted their gods with wings. Descriptions of the Batsquatch bear a striking resemblence to their god Anzu, shared by several Mesopotamian religions.

Linda pointed out that the same creature, or another like it, has been seen on the East Coast, too. Reports have come from Pennsylvania, Ohio, Missouri and elsewhere.

"A man in western Wisconsin had an encounter with a Batsquatch-like creature, and he was afraid it would run into his pickup-truck windshield," Linda told us. "The wingspread was at least as wide as the truck. At the last minute, it zipped up into the air and flew off.

"The common denominators here are that the creature was said to take off straight up, and that witnesses often became physically ill, sometimes for a few weeks," Linda said.

The Ear Eater of Jasper County

One of the oddest creatures in the American monster lexicon has to be the so-called Ear Eater of Jasper County, Mississippi. Fortunately, human ears didn't seem to be on the menu. It liked hogs. And nobody could see it.

"It terrorized nine different farms in this area for a few weeks in 1977," Linda Godfrey said. "It was after the pork population. Whatever it was, it had jaws big enough and strong enough to bite the head off a 50-pound hog."

The creature even tried to decapitate a 300-pound sow, but only tore away the ears, earning it its scary nickname.

"It left large, dog-like tracks and was never caught," Linda stated.

We can find no further reports of this creature, so there's no telling what it was or where it went.

A Tough-Toothed Lizardman in South Carolina

The Ear Eater has nothing on the South Carolina Lizardman, who apparently tried to eat a car.

Lee County sheriff's deputies arrived at a rural home near Bishopville on July 14, 1988, to find severe damage to a car that had been on Tom and Mary Waye's property all night. There were teeth marks, reddish-brown fur and muddy footprints on the car, the antenna was broken, and each side of the car was scratched. The hood had been torn open and some of the engine wires appeared to have been chewed by a large animal.

A common conception of Lizardman, as depicted by artist Karin Mansberg.

The first actual Lizardman sighting we know of took place about 18 miles away and nearly a month earlier, when a young man was driving home from work near Scape Ore Swamp, an enormous wilderness area near Sumter, about halfway between the state capital, Columbia, and Myrtle Beach on the coast.

The witness, Christopher Davis, 17 at the time, had a blowout on a lonely road near the swamp, and he had to change the tire. According to him, he heard a noise behind him as he finished changing the tire, turned around with his flashlight, and there was a frightening creature with dark hair all over its husky body, about seven feet tall, and with scales on its bizarre face, three-fingered hands and three-toed feet. It was running toward him across a field.

Petrified, Davis jumped into the car, started it, and took off. But not before the creature leaped onto the car roof, grasping both sides in an effort to stay on. Davis finally swerved enough to throw Lizardman off, but not before whatever it was damaged the car with scratch marks and broken side mirrors.

Some later eyewitnesses said that Lizardman had a tail.

Davis stayed mum about his sighting until other reports started coming in, notably the story of the damaged car in Bishopville. From nearby Browntown, witnesses talked about a similar creature, this one with red eyes.

There were enough credible reports of the creature to convince the Sheriff's Department that people were seeing something that was probably dangerous. Biologists told them that the hair samples were difficult, if not impossible, to identify. Officials did make casts of what were believed to be the creature's tracks, which were about 14 inches long and, indeed, three-toed.

Johnny Evans of the South Carolina Marine Resources Department was quoted as saying that the tracks weren't those of any known animal.

Lizard Liaison

In the mid-1990s, two different reports of an apparent lizardman came from State Highway 13 in Wisconsin on the same day.

One was filed by a state game warden, of all people. He was driving along in broad daylight when he suddenly spotted someone standing in the road. According to the officer, this turned out to be a "shiny," winged humanoid with green scales. The creature suddenly soared straight up, then over the vehicle, landing in the road behind.

A short time later and a short distance down the road, a highway crew was on the way to their work area in a truck, and apparently saw the same creature, describing it in the same way: a green, shiny, lizard-like man who flew into the trees and out of sight.

The Owlman

At Mawnan, in southern Cornwall, England, on April 17, 1976, two young girls reported seeing the Mothman-like creature that would become known as the Cornish Owlman. People who weren't there soon dismissed this as a large barn owl that must have been living in a nearby church tower. In fact, the girls said they saw a huge "feathered bird-man" hovering over that very tower.

The case was investigated by British researcher Anthony Shiels, who considered the girls credible. There was another sighting three months later in the same location, and there were sporadic reports of Owlman's sights and sounds through the rest of the century.

Reports generally described the creature as man-sized, and often with "glowing eyes and black, pincer-like claws."

The Jersey Devil

While many people have heard of the Jersey Devil, and he even has a professional hockey team named after him, they might not be aware of the creature's long history and scary appearances, and that he "attacked" the suburbs of Philadelphia in January 1909.

Before one *Behind the Paranormal* broadcast in 2016, a listener from Cape May, New Jersey, wrote in with has grandmother's story of a black, horse-like face that looked in her window...her second-floor window. There was no sign of any wings flapping, she said.

Rumors of a strange, demonic flying creature in and around the New Jersey Pine Barrens or Pinelands have been heard since the 1700s. The Pine Barrens themselves are a 1,700 square-mile wilderness area on the coastal plain, still largely rural and undisturbed even though it's in the middle of the thickly-settled Northeast Corridor of the United States, practically within sight of New York City.

Despite his long legend, the Devil certainly had his day in 1909, when he was reported in at least 30 communities in New Jersey and adjacent Pennsylvania.

"I looked from the window and was astonished to see a large creature standing on the banks of the (Delaware) canal. It looked something like an eagle...and it hopped along the tow-path," the press quoted homeowner John McOwen as saying.

McOwen's sighting was at about 2 a.m. on January 17.

Also reporting a winged creature hopping around Bristol that night was police officer James Sackville, who noted that it had "strange features and a horrible scream."

Sackville said that he ran toward the creature and, being a good, early 20th century man, tried to shoot it, but it flew away.

The Jersey Devil, presumably, was also seen in Bristol early that morning by none other than the postmaster, E.W. Minster, who said it was flying over the

One of the most common conceptions of flying cryptids such as the Jersey Devil, as depicted by artist Karin Mansberg.

Delaware River. He said it seemed to be glowing.

Other descriptions from that strange period give the creature a long, thick neck, the horned head of a goat or ram, with long, thin wings and stumpy legs. Its cry was variously described as a scream, a whistle or a squawk.

Indeed, the Jersey Devil, or what people thought was him, seemed to be on an early spring fling, stirring up a hullabaloo and being seen by perhaps hundreds of people.

A few days after the Bristol sightings, on January 19, a couple in Gloucester City, New Jersey, watched the creature cavorting on the roof of their barn for 10 to 15 minutes.

"It was about three feet and a half high, with a head like a collie dog and a face like a horse," the homeowner, Nelson Evans, told reporters later. "It had a long neck, wings about two feet long, and its back legs were like those of a crane, and it had horse's hooves."

According to Evans, the creature walked on its hind legs. Its front legs were short and had paws.

"It didn't use the front legs at all while we were watching. My wife and I were scared, I tell you, but I managed to open the window and say 'shoo!' and it turned around, barked at me, and flew away."

Descriptions from other witnesses talked about scaly or alligator-like skin, and a much greater height, six feet or more.

The final major reports from this Jersey Devil flap came on January 22, after which the creature seems to have disappeared into the Pine Barrens once again.

There are still occasional sightings, but nothing like the ruckus that took place in 1909.

Anything Weird that Flies

"Flying cryptids can be bizarre creatures that range all the way from giant birds to things that don't look like birds at all," said Linda Godfrey during one her appearances on *Behind the Paranormal*. "They can also be winged humanoids. It's a constantly-evolving list of creatures and entities, and we don't know what they are."

The bird-like ones can come in all varieties, Linda told us.

"Some look like great storks, others like raptors (eagles or hawks), giant owls, buzzards…everything up to and including extinct pterosaurs."

The typical reported wingspan is 10 to 20 feet, Linda stated.

The Webb Lake Big Bird

"I investigated a bizarre report in 2005 from a professional businessman from Minneapolis who was vacationing in northwestern Wisconsin, not far from the

Mississippi River," said Linda. "I think it's one of the best sighting reports of a birdlike cryptid I've ever seen."

Most of the time, she explained, witnesses don't get a look at a creature more than once.

"It's notoriously difficult to estimate the size of something in the sky unless there's something next to it to provide scale. This creature was seen in daylight, at close range."

It was about 11 a.m. on a lovely June morning in 2005. John Bolduan, 45 years old and over six feet tall, was riding his bicycle.

"He looked over into a grassy meadow, and there, standing in the grass, was a giant bird," Linda said. "It was stork-like and silvery white to pale gray in color. The man realized that the bird was quite a bit taller than he was, and he felt like he'd just come across something from a fantasy theme park, like a miracle."

Bolduan dismounted and started walking into the field.

"He did that without even thinking, because he was so fascinated. Then he thought this might be a female guarding a nest or something, and he got this sinking feeling."

Then the bird turned and looked at Bolduan.

"It started flapping and appeared to try to fly away," Linda said. "But it had trouble at that size moving its wings at a speed that would get it into the air."

We found this interesting. If it had stumbled across a brane, or world boundary, from somewhere or somewhen where the laws of physics, or even the gravity, were a little different, it might have weighed more here than it did there, hence the trouble getting into the air. As Linda described it, this giant bird didn't seem to feel at home.

"It finally managed to take off," said Linda. "The witness said he could see the feather structure billowing as it did so."

Linda was convinced that this was no hallucination.

"It was 100 percent 3-D, and he watched it fly toward a road he'd been cycling on. It was an asphalt road that led through a nice area of vacation homes," Linda noted. "It followed the roadway for a while, but he was able to see that the wings stretched from one side of the road to the other."

When Linda interviewed Bolduan on-site, the road turned out to be about 22 feet wide.

"So this thing had a 22-foot wingspan."

As with many who see cryptids, Bolduan considered this experience a life milestone. He wanted to know why he was singled out to see this.

The Black Hawk Connection

"I came across a story of an island a little farther down the Mississippi from

The Thunderbird, seen here atop a totem pole in Thunderbird Park in Victoria, British Columbia, Canada, is a common figure in First Nations belief. Bob C/Shutterstock

this sighting, where Chief Black Hawk of the Black Hawk War (1832) went as a young man, before the tribe had to move," Linda recalled. "It was a beautiful hunting place, and a great white spirit bird lived on the island and protected it."

After the tribe was forced to leave, so did the bird, according to the legend.

"This is fanciful on my part, of course, but the natives might have known about the same species this man saw in 2005, and thought it was a spirit creature."

Linda pointed out that sightings of giant birds in states bordering the Mississippi River really took off in the 1960s.

"This is when they started putting highways through the rain forests of South America. So, I wonder if this activity dislodged creatures who had found their last refuge in those South American forests, many of which are very dense," Linda speculated.

"Suddenly, there's a larger population of humans, and the creatures may have flown north. That could have been part of an explanation for some of this."

The Van Meter Visitor

No-one has ever identified the Van Meter Visitor - a huge, winged creature with a glowing horn that terrified Van Meter, Iowa, for several nights in 1903. Supposedly, whatever it was flew out of an abandoned mine, the sort of place many cryptid researchers suggest might be a refuge for all kinds of mysterious creatures.

Regardless of where it came from, the Van Meter Visitor was seen by virtually the entire population. It was described as a half human, half animal with enormous bat wings and, in one of the oddest characteristics ever attributed to a cryptid, had a blinding light shooting from its horn.

People would shoot at it, with no effect.

Eventually, in a picture reminiscent of the final scene from the 1956 Japanese monster flick *Rodan*, the townspeople chased the creature back to its mine-shaft, only to be confronted by a second one. Both creatures disappeared down the mine shaft and were never seen again, so the tale goes.

Making the best of the situation, Van Meter throws an annual festival to celebrate the incidents.

Back to the Multiverse Yet Again?

At this point, we can't help but return to the idea of intersects among parallel worlds with different laws of physics and different kinds of inhabitants.

Only one of the many questions that arise: Why do some flying cryptids not flap their wings when they takeoff?

"It is strange," Linda agreed. "The Wisconsin Man Bat, for example, was about to hit someone's windshield. It just spread its wings and soared upward into the trees."

EPILOGUE

Just about everyone interested in the paranormal field thinks the government, or something that looks like the government, is hushing up what they know about UFOs. But is information about cryptids, especially Bigfoot, being hushed up also?

Nick Redfern had some thoughts on that during one of his appearances on *Behind the Paranormal with Paul & Ben Eno.*

"That's one of the most controversial questions in cryptozoology," said Nick, who believes that U.S. federal authorities might even be in possession of Bigfoot bodies.

"In May 1980, the huge eruption of Mount St. Helens took place in Washington State. The blast flattened roughly 200 square miles of forest. The pyroclastic flow traveled at 250 mph. Sixty people were killed."

Military personnel were among the first responders.

"That was to be expected. But, in a matter of months, 15 retired military people came forward with knowledge about Bigfoot having been found dead on the mountain," Nick revealed.

"The natives always had legends of large, hairy people who lived on Mount St. Helens. Now there were military helicopters with nets hanging down, and soldiers on the ground loading large, hairy creatures," he added. "They were probably flown to a base."

We are still tracking down these stories, and it's difficult to find anything but second-hand information.

At the meeting of a Bigfoot organization a few years ago, there were reports of two Sasquatch bodies removed from the area by the Army Corps of Engineers, and two other bodies on the banks of the Cowlitz River. We're still looking for reports and witnesses.

If cryptids are being kept secret, then what for? Why would a strictly zoological mystery have anything to do with national security? It might have every-

A Washington National Guard helicopter flies over the scene of devastation at Mount St. Helens in May 1980. *Courtesy Washington Military Department*

thing to do with it if what we suggest is true: That the nature of reality, the kind of world we live in and the kind of beings we are, has little to do with what we see around us.

"When we have links between Bigfoot sightings and UFO activity, when we have either one appearing or vanishing in a flash of light, and when we have things that apparently straddle the flesh-and-blood world and others, we have something that pushes cryptids away from the ordinary animal world," Nick said.

We ourselves have seen overwhelming evidence that the government, corporate interests, or whoever else keeps the secrets, is well aware that we live in an interactive multiverse where time and space are simultaneous. They already know, and have known for perhaps 150 years or more, that aliens, cryptids and people's worst nightmares (and their most beautiful dreams) are not far away on some other planet, or in some novel or storybook, but right next to us all the time.

Think of the power that would come from weaponizing the paranormal, from appeared to be able to control time, space…and minds.

"The military is less interested in Bigfoot than it is in how they come and go from our reality," Nick agreed.

"I'm convinced that Bigfoot isn't just an unknown American ape. He seems to have UFO overtones, paranormal overtones, and this is what interests official agencies," he added.

"If Bigfoot, as some of the evidence suggests, flits in and out of a paranormal reality, they would want to know what technology or process is used to jump from this reality to another, or to distort time and space. That would give whoever possessed that technology some incredible advantages over an enemy. So I think that's why Bigfoot is secretly watched and studied."

In fact, Freedom of Information Act (FOIA) documents indicate a definite CIA interest in Bigfoot. Nick told us about U.S. State Department documents from the late 1940s.

"They're guidelines on how to handle an encounter with a Tibetan Yeti, based on legislation by the Tibetan Government," Nick said. "Yeti were not to be approached as if they were animals. The files are actually worded as if the Yeti's existence had already been verified, which is very interesting. They were told not to shoot unless they felt their lives were threatened."

Of great interest is the fact that all photos of Yeti had to be handed over to the Tibetan Government. Presumably, this all ended when China took over Tibet in 1950, and all related documents are undoubtedly under wraps in Beijing.

Should we be afraid?

When it comes to the paranormal in general and cryptids in particular, especially when they have fangs and glowing red eyes, should we fear for our safety?

If the multiverse scenario is true, what's to stop Godzilla or King Bigfoot from crashing through a brane and eating New York?

All we can do is agree with Linda Godfrey when she suggested that there seem to be limits, and even some unwritten rules, on what cryptids can do. This could be because they are never entirely across the brane into our world and we are never entirely into theirs.

Looking at the cases, especially when it comes to Bigfoot, we notice two things. First, hostile action against humans seems to occur only when we heavily violate their territory, as in large logging operations. Second, cryptid experiences almost always seem entirely unexpected. It's as though they find us. We can testify to that first-hand.

"There are reports of Bigfoot attacking loggers over the course of several nights in northern California in 1924," Nick told us.

It wasn't as if the Bigfeet didn't have good reason. The miners claimed they had shot a Bigfoot the day before, only to have their cabin pelted with dirt, rocks and debris throughout the following nights. Interestingly, the area is known as Ape Canyon to this day.

That same year, a Canadian, Albert Ostman, alleged that he was abducted by a Bigfoot and was held captive by its entire family for six days before he could escape.

Another story of an assault by Bigfoot came from Chesterfield, Ohio, where, in 1902, some ice skaters reported being attacked by a hairy, eight-foot creature that carried a wooden stick.

In the 1800s, a Bigfoot reportedly frightened off the entire population of Thompson's Flat, Oregon, except for one man, who was later found dead because of trauma to the head.

More recently, Bigfoot supposedly ripped up a California campground in the 1970s, killing people. As the story goes, the government kept a lid on this story, until it was leaked in a newsletter of unknown veracity in the early 1990s.

Albert Rosales probably said it best. "With Bigfoot, some are hostile, some are peaceful. It probably depends on the attitude you bring with you."

Has mainstream science loosened up on cryptids?

"Not really," said Nick Redfern. "For one thing, zoologists often have the attitude: 'I'm the expert. Don't talk to me about monsters!' Secondly, we're up against the fact that scientists don't want to do anything to jeopardize their grants from universities, corporations and organizations."

They just don't want to rock the boat, according to Nick.

"I view that as a cowardly way out of facing what might be uncomfortable. I've often spoken to these people, and they admit there might be something to this, but there's no way they will go on the record about it."

We agree with Nick that the problem isn't science, it's scientists who consider themselves priests of accepted truth rather than questioners of it.

Talk to the animals

In the Cold War era, the defense establishments in both the United States and the Soviet Union weren't reluctant to push the scientific envelope.

"As an offshoot of its studies about militarizing remote viewing and psychic spying in humans, Russia had a program of government-funded animal extra-sensory perception (ESP) research," Nick told us. "If they could understand how it worked in animals, they thought they could understand how it worked in people."

Trouble is, human ESP doesn't seem to work all the time.

"Defense Intelligence Agency (DIA) files from the 1970s discuss what the Russians had been doing since the 1920s with research into mind-to-mind contact between dogs and humans," Nick said. "A person would psychically project a command to a dog, and the dog would do it."

The Soviets even tried psychic experiments to see if animals had souls and life after death, according to Nick.

"They did a grisly experiment with rabbits. They would separate the mother from the babies, then destroy them one by one (in a different room) with the mother wired with electrodes. According to official records, the mother would have notable reactions, as if she knew each time a baby rabbit was destroyed. It's disturbing, yet fascinating."

The real questions for us are: Can we communicate with cryptids, and do we even know if and when they try to communicate with us? And more significantly, have governments or other powers-that-be learned to communicate with cryptids?

Does it really depend on who's looking?

During one of her many appearances on the show, Ben asked Linda Godfrey how much culture, popular perception and individual preconceptions play into cryptid experiences.

Linda told us about a colleague who believed that cryptid experiences aren't individualized at all, but are part of some pervasive spirit-matrix that can interact with individual humans and show itself as any number of creatures.

"This matrix can interact with human consciousness, almost like a quantum computer, as some physicists might say," Linda responded. "It uses whatever is in that person's mind to serve its own purpose."

Linda said she saw what could be an example of this while working on her book *Haunted Michigan.*

"The owner of a local museum took me to the basement and turned off the light. At the same time, we both saw a basketball-sized, light-emitting sphere," she recalled. "It was about seven feet away, near the ceiling."

Interestingly, the sphere evaporated as soon as Linda pulled up her camera to take a picture.

The staff at the museum called this apparition "Basement Billy," Linda said, noting that another visitor had seen the full specter of a person, not just a ball of light.

"I had no expectations or preconceptions," Linda said. "I just saw a ball of energy. Maybe that's how it is with cryptids."

"Does that make the experience more real or less real?" Ben asked.

"It was certainly a real experience to me and to the lady," Linda replied. "I could scarcely believe it was there! I felt that it had awareness and was curious about me. I've since had other experiences with light spheres."

Nice Doggie

Paul asked Linda if she'd heard reports from people who have had very positive experiences with cryptids, perhaps because they had very positive outlooks in general.

"Yes, but that's very much in the minority," Linda responded. "Most people who see a giant, unknown creature are terrified. They'll say, 'I wish I'd never seen it!' The experience preys on people's minds. I've run into that with people who have seen the unknown upright canines."

Linda cited one example of a relatively positive cryptid experience.

"One lady told me she was driving through a cornfield to bring lunch to her farmer husband. She saw an upright canine cryptid passing through the corn-rows, and it stopped to look at her. She said she was not afraid. In fact, she felt fortunate. She knew that it was peaceful, and wasn't going to hurt her."

Perhaps Wahabah Hadia al Mu'id summed it up best.

"We live amidst an embarrassingly glorious exuberance of life. We're still learning about ourselves, and we have so much to learn about the other beings with whom we share this planet."

Bibliography

ALTEN, Steve. *MEG: A Novel of Deep Terror (1st Revised Edition)*. Cabot, Arkansas: Viper Press, 2015)

BELLAMY, Robin Pyatt. *Haunted Hospitality*. CreateSpace Independent Publishing, 2012

BURNETTE, Tom and RIGGS, Rob. Bigfoot: Exploring the Myth & Discovering the Truth. Woodbury, Minnesota: Llewellyn Publications, 2014.

CITRO, Joseph A. *Green Mountain Ghosts, Ghouls & Unsolved Mysteries*. New York: Mariner Books, 1994.

COLEMAN, Loren and HUYGHE, Patrick. T*he Field Guide To Bigfoot And Other Mystery Primates*. Charlottesville, Virginia: Anomalist Books, 2014.

COLEMAN, Loren. *Monsters of Massachusetts: Mysterious Creatures in the Bay State*. Mechanicsburg, Pennsylvania: Stackpole Books, 2013.

COLEMAN, Loren. *Mysterious America: The Ultimate Guide to the Nation's Weirdest Wonders, Strangest Spots, and Creepiest Creatures*. New York: Gallery Books, 2007

COLEMAN, Loren. *Bigfoot!: The True Story of Apes in America*. New York: Paraview Books, 2003.

COLEMAN, Loren and HUYGHE, Patrick. *The Field Guide to Lake Monsters, Sea Serpents and Other Mystery Denizens of the Deep*. New York: TarcherPerigee, 2003.

COLEMAN, Loren. *Mothman and Other Curious Encounters (3rd Edition)*. New York: Paraview Books, 2002.

COLEMAN, Loren. *Tom Slick: True Life Encounters in Cryptozoology*. Fresno, California: Craven Street Books, 2002.

COLEMAN, Loren and CLARK, Jerome. *Cryptozoology A To Z: The Encyclopedia of Loch Monsters, Sasquatch, Chupacabras, and Other Authentic Mysteries of Nature*. New York: Simon and Schuster, 1999.

ENO, Paul and ENO, Ben. *Behind the Paranormal: Everything You Know is Wrong*. Atglen, Pennsylvania: Schiffer Books, 2016.

ENO, Paul F. *Turning Home: God, Ghosts and Human Destiny*. Woonsocket, Rhode Island: New River Press, 2006.

FREEMAN, Richard Alan. *Dragons: More than a Myth*. Bideford, Devon: CFZ Publishing, 2005.

FREEMAN, Richard. *Orang Pendek: Sumatra's Forgotten Ape*. Bideford, Devon: CFZ Publishing, 2011.

FREEMAN, Richard. *The Great Yokai Encyclopaedia: The A-Z of Japanese Monsters*. Bideford, Devon: CFZ Publishing, 2010.

GODFREY, Linda S. *Monsters Among Us: An Exploration of Otherworldly Bigfoots, Wolfmen, Portals, Phantoms, and Odd Phenomena*. New York: TarcherPerigee, 2016.

GODFREY, Linda S. *The Beast of Bray Road: Tailing Wisconsin's Werewolf*. New York: Dystel & Goderich Literary Management, 2015.

GODFREY, Linda S. *American Monsters: A History of Monster Lore, Legends, and Sightings in America*. New York: TarcherPerigee, 2014.

GODFREY, Linda S. *Real Wolfmen: True Encounters in Modern America*. New York: TarcherPerigee, 2012.

GODFREY, Linda S. *Haunted Wisconsin: Ghosts and Strange Phenomena of the Badger State*. New York: Stackpole Books, 2010.

GODFREY, Linda S. *The Michigan Dogman: Werewolves and Other Unknown Canines Across the U.S.A.* Eau Claire, Wisconsin: Unexplained Research Publishing, 2010.

GODFREY, Lina S. *Lake and Sea Monsters (Mysteries, Legends, and Unexplained Phenomena)*. New York: Chelsea House Publishing, 2008.

GODFREY, Linda S. *Werewolves: Mysteries, Legends, and Unexplained Phenomena*. New York: Checkmark Books, 2008.

GODFREY, Linda S. *Hunting the American Werewolf*. Black Earth, Wisconsin: Trails Media Group, 2006.

GODFREY, Linda S. *Weird Michigan: Your Travel Guide to Michigan's Local Legends and Best Kept Secrets*. New York: Sterling Books, 2006.

HILLING, Jeff. *Bigfoot Booyah* (E-book). Barnes & Noble Nook, 2013.

HILLING, Jeff. *American Bigfoot* (E-book). Barnes & Noble Nook, 2013.

HILLING, Jeff. *The Great Bigfoot Film Mystery* (E-book). Barnes & Noble Nook, 2011.

LE BLANC, Ronny. *Monsterland: Encounters with UFOs, Bigfoot and Orange Orbs*. Anaheim, California: Blue Tiger Publishing, 2016.

REDFERN, Nick. *The Roswell UFO Conspiracy: Exposing A Shocking And Sinister Secret*. Bracey, Virginia: Lisa Haga Books, 2017.

REDFERN, Nick. *Monster Files: A Look Inside Government Secrets and Classified Documents on Bizarre Creatures and Extraordinary Animals*. Wayne, New Jersey: New Page Books, 2013.

REDFERN, Nick. *Keep Out!: Top Secret Places Governments Don't Want You to Know About*. Wayne, New Jersey: New Page Books, 2011.

REDFERN, Nick. *The Real Men In Black: Evidence, Famous Cases, and True Stories of These Mysterious Men and their Connection to UFO Phenomena.* Wayne, New Jersey: New Page Books, 2011.

REDFERN, Nick. *There's Something in the Woods.* Charlottesville, Virginia: Anomalist Books, 2008.

REDFERN, Nick. *Memoirs of a Monster Hunter: A Five-Year Journey in Search of the Unknown.* Wayne, New Jersey: New Page Books, 2007.

REDFERN, Nick. *Three Men Seeking Monsters: Six Weeks in Pursuit of Werewolves, Lake Monsters, Giant Cats, Ghostly Devil Dogs, and Ape-Men.* New York: Gallery Books, 2004.

RIGGS, Rob. *In the Big Thicket: On the Trail of the Wild Man : Exploring Nature's Mysterious Dimension.* New York: Paraview Press, 2001.

ROBINSON, Jeremy. *Kronos.* Cabot, Arkansas: Variance Publishing, 2009.

ROSALES, Albert S. *UFOs over Florida: Humanoid and other Strange Encounters in the Sunshine State.* CreateSpace Independent Publishing, 2017.

ROSALES, Albert S. *Humanoid Encounters: The Others Amongst Us* (Series of 16 books). CreateSpace Independent Publishing.

SHEPPARD, Susan. *Cry of the Banshee: History and Hauntings of West Virginia and the Ohio Valley.* Charleston, West Virginia: Quarrier Press, 2008.

SPENCER, Philip. *The Wildman of Kentucky: The Mystery of Panther Rock.* Foresthill, California: Reality Press, 2008.

WAMSLEY, Jeff and SARGENT, Donnie Jr. *Mothman: The Facts Behind the Legend.* Proctorville, Ohio: Mark S. Phillips Publishing, 2002.

WAMSLEY, Jeff. *Mothman: Behind the Red Eyes.* Point Pleasant, West Virginia: Mothman Press, 2005.

ZARZYNSKI, Joseph. *Champ: Beyond the Legend* (Updated Edition). Salt Lake City, Utah: MZ Publishing, 1988.

The Authors: Paul & Ben Eno

Paul (left) & Ben Eno are best known as the father-son co-hosts of the CBS Radio and WOON 1240 Boston/Worcester/Providence Sunday destination show *Behind the Paranormal*, with an estimated three million listeners. They have nearly 60 years of combined experience as paranormal researchers and adventurers. This is the second book they have written together.

Paul was one of the first paranormal investigators of the early 1970s, beginning while he was studying for the priesthood. His early mentors included parapsychology pioneer Dr. Louisa Rhine, Fr. John J. Nicola S.J. (technical advisor for the film *The Exorcist*) and legendary, first-generation "ghost hunters" Ed & Lorraine Warren.

He graduated from two seminaries, but was expelled from a third because of his paranormal work with less than two years to go before ordination. He ended up as an award-winning New England journalist and the author of six books on the paranormal and two books on history. Paul and his wife, Jackie, live in Woonsocket, Rhode Island.

*

Ben joined his dad's adventures in 2005 at the age of 13, demonstrating some unique insights and, at 16, becoming the youngest syndicated broadcaster in America. Ben is a sound expert and a graduate of Emerson College in Boston with a degree in sound design and audio post-production.

Ben and his wife, Marian, live in Milford, Massachusetts.

The Illustrator: Karin Mansberg

Karin Mansberg is an illustrator and printmaker, and enjoys teaching block printing. She was born is Estonia, a country with many lakes, forests and a population of only about a million people. Her prints and drawings explore connections between observed (nature), remembered (childhood memories of being in nature), and imagined (landscapes). She prints on fabric and paper, alternating controlled, designed marks with spontaneous processes of monotype, collage and drawing.

Karin studied art history and criticism at the Estonian Academy of Art in Tallinn (1996-1999). However, later she realized that she preferred hands-on experiences in art and, after moving to the United States, studied art and printmaking at Western Connecticut State University (2007-2013), graduating with the MFA in illustration.

You can follow her creative journey on Instagram: @karin.mansberg or Facebook: / BLOCKprintedArt

---

Other Books by Paul & Ben Eno

Behind the Paranormal:
Everything You Know is Wrong
(Schiffer Books, November 2016)

Books by Paul F. Eno

Turning Home:
God, Ghosts and Human Destiny
(New River Press, 2006)

Rhode Island: A Genial History
(New River Press, 2005)

Footsteps in the Attic:
More First-Hand Accounts of the Paranormal in New England
(New River Press, 2002)

Faces at the Window:
First Hand Accounts of the Paranormal in Southern New England
(New River Press, 1998)

American National Biography (Contributor): William Blackstone
(Oxford University Press, 1988)

Acknowledgements

To our friends, colleagues and guests on *Behind the Paranormal with Paul & Ben Eno* over the years, without whose interviews this book wouldn't have been possible.

Steve Alten
Robin Pyatt Bellamy
The late Nigel Brierly
Tom Burnette
Loren Coleman
Richard Freeman
Linda Godfrey
Jeff Hilling
Ronny Le Blanc
Wahabah Hadia al Mu'id
The late Rob Riggs
Jeremy Robinson
Albert Rosales
Susan Sheppard
Shane Sirois
The late Philip Spencer
Jeff Wamsley

To our talented and generous illustrator, Karin Mansberg. And to our friends who provided graphics of their own, Linda Godfrey Albert Rosales and Jeff Wamsley.

We also thank Peter Schiffer of Schiffer Books, our usual publisher, for graciously tweaking our contract so that we could get this book out on time for our summer events by using our own media company's imprint.

To Jackie, Paul's wife of 36 years, and Marian, Ben's wife of one year, for their patience as we run around the country, chasing monsters and signing books.

And to the folks without whose support our show, now entering its 10th year, wouldn't be possible: WOON 1240 Station Managers Dave Richards & Denise LePage, Tech Producer Craig Pelletier, Executive Producer Josh Ducharme, Online Producer Marian Eno, and Casting Producer Lori Greer.

Check out the first book in this series!

Behind the Paranormal: Everything You Know is Wrong

Journey through the paranormal from prehistory to the planets and our future, with over 50 bizarre cases of ghosts, poltergeists, demons, cryptids, UFOs, and other out-of-the-ordinary phenomena. Based on CBS and WOON 1240 radio scripts broadcast by a world-famous father-and-son team of paranormal investigators, their research has revealed bizarre connections not only between seemingly unrelated occurrences but also between the paranormal and our everyday lives, the history of our species, and our possible future as a race. Meet inter-world parasites that might be farming your family or community, encounter disappearing buildings, and ghosts of people who aren't dead. Push the boundaries as you find out what the Bible and other ancient documents might really mean, and what UFOs, invisible friends, and those footsteps in the attic could really be. Explaining the paranormal is not the problem. It's handling the explanations. Everything you know is wrong.

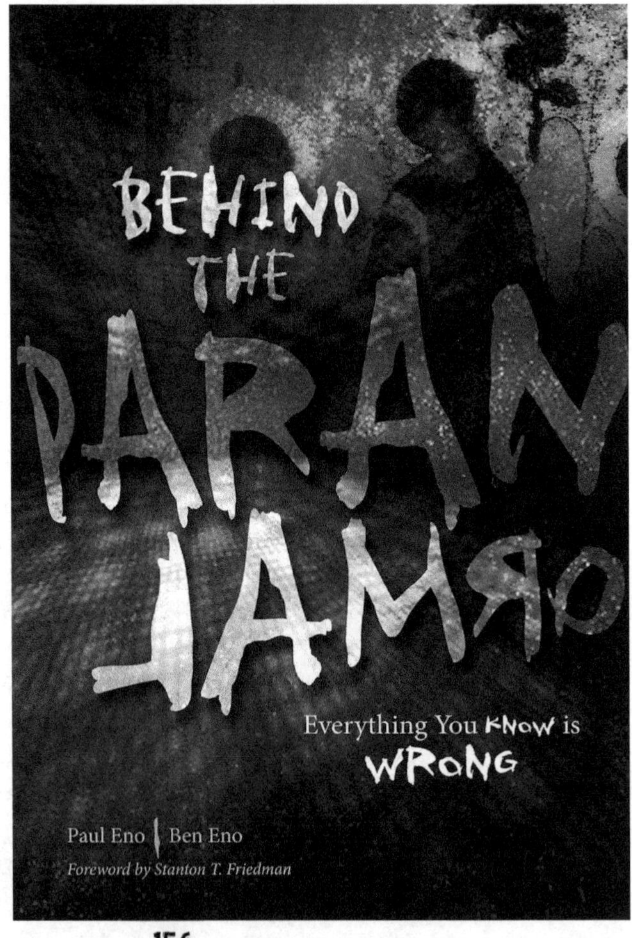

Publisher:
Schiffer Books, 2016
ISBN: 978-0764352-22-5
Paperback: 176 Pages
Suggested Retail Price: ($16.99 US)
Available from online retailers or your favorite bookstore.

Visit Amazon.com, Barnesandnoble.com or other online retailers for other books by Paul F. Eno from New River Press. For autographed copies, visit Behindtheparanormal.com.

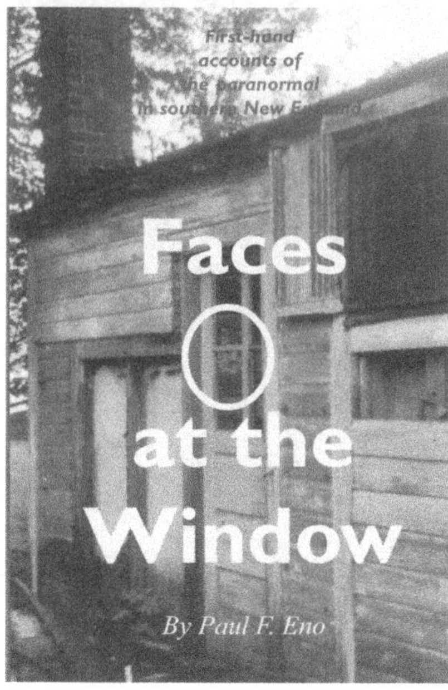

Visit the

International Cryptozoology Museum

Portland, Maine

Cryptozoologymuseum.com/

Visit the
Mothman Museum

Point Pleasant, West Virginia

Mothmanlives.com/

CPSIA information can be obtained
at www.ICGtesting.com
Printed in the USA
BVHW041254150821
614465BV00017B/1509

9 781891 724206